Taste of Home's

SLOW COOKER
FAVORITES

Editor: Faithann Stoner
Executive Editor/Books: Heidi Reuter Lloyd
Food Editor: Janaan Cunningham
Associate Food Editors: Coleen Martin, Diane Werner
Senior Recipe Editor: Sue A. Jurack
Recipe Editor: Janet Briggs
Associate Editors: Beth Wittlinger, Julie Schnittka,
Jean Steiner, Susan Uphill
Graphic Art Associates: Ellen Lloyd, Catherine Fletcher
Food Photography: Rob Hagen, Dan Roberts,
Jim Wieland
Set Stylist: Sue Myers

Senior Vice President, Editor in Chief: Catherine Cassidy
President: Barbara Newton
Chairman and Founder: Roy Reiman

©2005 Reiman Media Group, Inc.
5400 S. 60th Street, Greendale, WI 53129
International Standard Book Number:
0-89821-459-9
Library of Congress Control Number:
2005931971
Printed in China.
Second Printing, December 2006

CONTENTS

Slow Cookers Put You on The Fast Track for Fixing Dinner

If you think you can't put a wholesome supper on the table when busy days keep you out of the kitchen, think again! Slow cookers provide unbeatable fix-it-and-forget-it convenience, so you can offer from-scratch fare even on your most hurried days.

Just fill your slow cooker early in the day, turn it on and head out the door. When you come home, you'll be greeted with the wonderful aroma of a simmering dish. By planning ahead, you save time when you need it most.

Best of all, with only one dirty pot, cleanup is a breeze. And if you can't handle the heat in the kitchen, using a slow cooker keeps it cool!

You'll quickly be on your way to enjoying the benefits of slow cooking with *Taste of Home's Slow Cooker Favorites*. This book is chock-full of 238 great-tasting recipes from past issues of *Taste of Home* magazine and its "sister" publications, so it's a snap to prepare entrees, soups, side dishes, appetizers…even dessert!

You can make every dish with confidence because each one is a tried-and-true favorite of a fellow busy cook. Plus, each recipe has been prepared and taste-tested by our own kitchen staff.

Since some recipes cook all day, while others require only a few hours, we've prominently highlighted the cooking time for each recipe right under the recipe title. You can easily select recipes that fit your schedule. (There's also a listing of recipes organized by cooking time starting on page 281 of the index.)

But before you plug in your slow cooker, turn to page 5 for information on making slow cooking even easier and more convenient. Whether you're a new or seasoned slow cooker user, you're sure to appreciate this handy section and the other helpful hints and tips throughout the book.

Soon you'll be enjoying many economical, nutritious and delicious dishes with minimal time and fuss.

This slow cooker's companion is one cookbook you'll turn to time and time again!

SLOW COOKER HINTS & TIPS

DIFFERENCE BETWEEN A CROCK-POT®
AND A SLOW COOKER

The original slow cooker, called a Crock-Pot, was introduced in 1971 by Rival®. The term "slow cooker" and the name Crock-Pot are frequently used interchangeably when referring to this appliance.

The most popular slow cookers have heat coils circling a crockery insert. With this type, the heat surrounds the food to help it cook evenly.

These models have two heat settings: "high" (equal to 300°F) and "low" (equal to 200°F).

Other types of slow cookers have heat coils on the bottom and have an adjustable thermostat.

All the recipes in this cookbook refer to cooking on either "high" or "low" for a certain amount of time.

When a range in cooking time is provided with a recipe, this accounts for variables such as thickness of meat, how full the slow cooker is, temperature of the food going into the cooker, etc.

As you become more familiar with your slow cooker, you'll be better able to judge which end of the range to use for cooking food.

A handy attribute of slow cookers is that if you can't get home at exactly the time the food should be done, it generally doesn't hurt to leave the slow cooker cooking on low for an extra hour.

SELECTING THE RIGHT SLOW COOKER SIZE

Slow cookers come in a range of sizes, from 1 quart to 6 quarts. It's important to use the right size for the amount of food you're making.

To cook properly and safely, manufacturers and the USDA recommend slow cookers be filled at least half full but no more than two-thirds full.

Check the chart below right to find the proper size slow cooker for you.

In general, to serve a dip from a buffet, the smallest slow cookers are ideal. To entertain or cook for a potluck dinner, the larger cookers work best.

Many slow cookers have a removable stoneware insert. That handy feature also allows you to assemble the food the night before, when it's convenient for you. Uncooked meats should be stored separately from other ingredients and added when you're ready to cook.

Cover and store the insert in the refrigerator. Then in the morning, you can just put in the insert, turn on the cooker and go.

Note: Don't preheat the base unit. An insert that has been in the refrigerator overnight should always be put into a cold base unit. Stoneware is sensitive to dramatic temperature changes and cracking or breakage could occur with preheating.

Another option, especially for recipes that require additional preparation like browning meat, is to assemble your recipe in the evening, put everything in the slow cooker and turn it on. Let it cook overnight while you sleep.

In the morning, when the recipe has cooked for the required amount of time, store your finished dish in the refrigerator and reheat it in the microwave at dinnertime.

Household Size	Size of Slow Cooker (in quarts)
1 person	1 to 1-1/2
2 people	2 to 3-1/2
3 or 4 people	3-1/2 to 4-1/2
4 or 5 people	4-1/2 to 5
6 or more people	5 to 6

Preparing Foods for the Slow Cooker

Meats. For enhanced flavor and appearance, meat may be browned before going into the slow cooker, but it's not necessary. If you decide not to brown the meat, you may want to add color when serving by sprinkling on chopped parsley or shredded cheese. Garnishes such as fresh herbs and lemon wedges can also help.

Vegetables. Vegetables, especially root vegetables like carrots and potatoes, tend to cook slower than meat. Place these vegetables on the bottom and around the sides of the slow cooker and put meat on top of the vegetables. Add tender vegetables like peas and zucchini, or those you'd prefer to be crisp-tender, during the last 15 to 60 minutes of cooking.

Dairy. Most milk-based products tend to break down during slow cooking. If possible, add items like milk, sour cream, cream cheese or cream during the last hour of cooking. Cheeses don't generally hold up over extended periods of cooking, so they should be added near the end of cooking—or use processed cheeses instead.

Seasonings. Whole herbs and spices are better than the crushed forms in the slow cooker. The whole berry or leaf is firmer and stands up better over long cooking times. They'll be at their peak at serving time. Add fresh herbs just before the end of cooking.

Beans. Dried beans can be tricky to work with in the slow cooker. Minerals in the water and variations in voltage affect different types of beans in different ways. As a result, dried beans should always be soaked before adding to a slow cooker recipe. Here's how:

Place beans in a Dutch oven or soup kettle; add water to cover by 2 inches. Bring to a boil; boil for 2 minutes. Remove from the heat; cover and let stand for 1 hour. Drain and rinse beans, discarding liquid.

Note: Lentils and split peas do not need to be soaked. After dried beans are completely cooked, they can be combined with sugar and/or acidic foods, such as tomato sauce. Sugar and acid have a hardening effect on beans and will prevent them from becoming tender. An alternative is to use canned beans that have been rinsed and drained.

Pasta. If added to a slow cooker when dry, pasta becomes very sticky. Partially cook pasta until it's almost tender but not completely cooked before adding. Or, boil it until completely tender and add it at the end of cooking just to heat it through and blend it with the other ingredients.

Fish. Fish is very tender and turns into flakes if slow cooked for long periods. Add fish during the last 20 minutes of cooking.

Slow Cooker Basics

- No peeking! Refrain from lifting the lid while the slow cooker is cooking unless you're instructed in a recipe to stir or add ingredients. The loss of steam can mean an additional 15 to 30 minutes of cooking time each time you lift the lid.
- Be sure the lid is seated properly—not tilted or askew. The steam during cooking creates a seal.
- Remove food from the slow cooker within 1 hour after it's finished cooking. Promptly refrigerate leftovers.
- Slow cooking may take longer at higher altitudes.

CONVERTING RECIPES FOR THE SLOW COOKER

Almost any recipe that bakes in the oven or simmers on the stovetop can be converted for the slow cooker. Here are some guidelines:

Using this book or the manufacturer's instruction booklet, locate a recipe similar to the one you want to convert. Use it as a guide. Note the quantity and size of meat and vegetable pieces, heat setting, cooking time and amount of liquid.

Note: Since there is no evaporation, foods tend to water down. If your recipe calls for 6 to 8 cups of water, you might want to start with 5 cups. Conversely, recipes should include some liquid. If a recipe doesn't include liquid, add 1/2 cup of water or broth.

In general, 1 hour of simmering on the range or baking at 350° F in the oven is equal to 8-10 hours on low or 4-5 hours on high in a slow cooker. Check the chart above.

Cooking Time for Conventional Recipe	Cooking Time in the Slow Cooker
15 to 30 minutes	Low: 4 to 6 hours
	High: 1-1/2 to 2 hours
35 to 45 minutes	Low: 6 to 8 hours
	High: 3 to 4 hours
50 minutes or more	Low: 8 to 10 hours
	High: 4 to 6 hours

Thickeners such as flour, cornstarch and tomato paste are used to give texture to foods cooked in the slow cooker.

Before converting recipes, check the manufacturer's guidelines for your particular slow cooker.

Helpful Foil Handles

1.

2.

3.

Meat loaves or layered dishes like Slow Cooker Enchiladas (p. 116) are easier to get out of the slow cooker using foil handles. Here's how:

1. Cut three 20- x 3-inch strips of heavy-duty aluminum foil or create them by folding wider strips of regular foil. Crisscross the strips so they resemble the spokes of a wheel. (See photo 1.)

2. Place the meat loaf in the center of the strips, and pull them up and bend the edges to form handles. (See photo 2.)

3. Grasp the foil handles to lift the loaf and lower it into the slow cooker. (See photo 3.) Leave the foil in while you cook so you can easily lift the meat out to serve.

Note: For a layered dish, place the strips in the cooker and up the sides before putting in the food. Leave them in. Once the food is cooked, pull the strips together as a handle to neatly remove the food in one piece.

CLEANING YOUR SLOW COOKER

Removable stoneware inserts make cleanup a breeze. Be sure to cool the insert before adding water for cleaning to avoid cracking.

Wash the insert in the dishwasher or in warm soapy water. Avoid using abrasive cleansers since they may scratch the stoneware.

To remove mineral stains on a crockery insert, fill the cooker with hot water and 1 cup white vinegar; cover. Turn heat control to high for 2 hours. Then empty. When cool, wash with hot sudsy water and a cloth or sponge. Rinse well and dry with a towel.

To remove water marks from a highly glazed crockery insert, rub the surface with vegetable oil and allow to stand for 2 hours before washing with hot sudsy water.

Do not immerse the metal base unit. Clean it with a damp sponge.

Check to See If Your Slow Cooker Works Properly

Did you inherit a used slow cooker or find one at a garage sale and want to see if it's working properly?

To be considered safe, a slow cooker must be able to cook slow enough so that it can be left unattended, yet it must be fast enough to keep the food at a safe temperature. Here's how to check:

1. Fill the slow cooker with 2 quarts of lukewarm water.

2. Heat on low with the lid covered for 8 hours.

3. Using a thermometer, check the temperature of the water quickly since the temperature can drop quite a bit once the lid is removed.

4. The temperature should be at 185° F. If it's too hot, your meal cooked for 8 hours would likely be overdone. If the temperature is below 185°, it could be the cooker does not heat food to an adequate temperature to avoid the growth of harmful bacteria.

SPECIAL USES

Don't forget your slow cooker when you go camping, provided electricity is available. It's a handy appliance when space is limited and you want "set-it-and-forget-it" meals.

Reheating foods in a slow cooker is not recommended. Cooked food can be brought to steaming on the stovetop or in the microwave and then put into a preheated slow cooker to keep hot for serving.

Use a slow cooker on a buffet table to keep soup, stew or mashed potatoes hot.

APPETIZERS & BEVERAGES

Taco Joe Dip

TACO JOE DIP

Cook Time: 5 to 7 Hours

1 can (16 ounces) kidney beans, rinsed and drained
1 can (15-1/4 ounces) whole kernel corn, drained
1 can (15 ounces) black beans, rinsed and drained
1 can (14-1/2 ounces) stewed tomatoes
1 can (8 ounces) tomato sauce
1 can (4 ounces) chopped green chilies, drained
1 envelope taco seasoning
1/2 cup chopped onion
Tortilla chips

In a slow cooker, combine the first eight ingredients. Cover and cook on low for 5-7 hours. Serve with tortilla chips. **Yield:** about 7 cups.

Editor's Note: To make Taco Joe Soup, add a 29-ounce can of tomato sauce to the slow cooker. It serves 6-8.

Lang Secrest
Sierra Vista, Arizona
This recipe was given to us by our daughter. My husband and I absolutely love it. Because it's conveniently prepared in a slow cooker, it's great for parties or busy days.

SLOW COOKER CHEESE DIP

Cook Time: 4 Hours

1 pound ground beef
1/2 pound bulk hot pork sausage
2 pounds process cheese (Velveeta), cubed
2 cans (10 ounces *each*) diced tomatoes and green chilies, undrained
Tortilla chips

In a skillet, cook beef and sausage over medium heat until no longer pink; drain. Transfer to a 5-qt. slow cooker. Add cheese and tomatoes; mix well.

Cover and cook on low for 4 hours or until the cheese is melted, stirring occasionally. Serve with tortilla chips. **Yield:** 3 quarts.

Marion Bartone
Conneaut, Ohio
I brought this spicy cheese dip to my quilt guild, where it was a huge hit. It's a terrific take-along appetizer.

Cheesy Pizza Fondue

CHEESY PIZZA FONDUE

Serve in Slow Cooker

1/2 pound ground beef
1 medium onion, chopped
2 cans (15 ounces *each*) pizza
    sauce
1-1/2 teaspoons dried basil *or*
    oregano
1/4 teaspoon garlic powder
2-1/2 cups (10 ounces) shredded
    sharp cheddar cheese
1 cup (4 ounces) shredded
    mozzarella cheese
Breadsticks

In a heavy saucepan, cook beef and onion over medium heat until meat is no longer pink; drain. Stir in the pizza sauce, basil and garlic powder; mix well.

Reduce heat to low. Add cheeses; stir until melted. Transfer to a slow cooker or fondue pot and keep warm over low heat. Serve with breadsticks. **Yield:** about 5 cups.

Julie Barwick
Mansfield, Ohio
While I was growing up, I would sit for hours reading cookbooks from cover to cover. I've carried that love of cooking with me through the years. I found this recipe when we lived in Wisconsin.

HEARTY BROCCOLI DIP

Cook Time: 2 to 3 Hours

1 pound ground beef
1 pound process cheese
    (Velveeta), cubed
1 can (10-3/4 ounces) condensed
    cream of mushroom soup,
    undiluted
1 package (10 ounces) frozen
    chopped broccoli, thawed
2 tablespoons salsa
Tortilla chips

In a skillet, cook beef over medium heat until no longer pink; drain. Transfer to a slow cooker. Add cheese, soup, broccoli and salsa; mix well.

Cover and cook on low for 2-3 hours or until heated through, stirring after 1 hour. Serve with tortilla chips. **Yield:** 5-1/2 cups.

Sue Call
Beech Grove, Indiana
You'll need just five ingredients to stir up this no-fuss appetizer. People often ask me to bring this creamy dip to potlucks.

SLOW-COOKED SALSA

Cook Time: 2-1/2 to 3 Hours

Toni Menard
Lompoc, California
I love the fresh taste of homemade salsa, but as a working mother, I don't have much time to make it. So I came up with this slow-cooked version that practically makes itself!

10 plum tomatoes, cored
2 garlic cloves
1 small onion, cut into wedges
2 jalapeno peppers
1/4 cup fresh cilantro
1/2 teaspoon salt
Tortilla chips

Cut a small slit in two tomatoes; insert a garlic clove into each slit. Place tomatoes and onion in a slow cooker. Cut stem off jalapenos; remove seeds if a milder salsa is desired. Place jalapenos in slow cooker. Cover and cook on high for 2-1/2 to 3 hours or until vegetables are softened (some may brown); cool.

In a blender or food processor, combine tomato mixture, cilantro and salt; cover and process until smooth. Serve with tortilla chips. **Yield:** about 2 cups.

Editor's Note: When cutting or seeding hot peppers, use rubber or plastic gloves to protect your hands. Avoid touching your face.

HOT CHILI DIP

Cook Time: 1 to 2 Hours

Nikki Rosati
Franksville, Wisconsin
I first made this zippy dip for my husband's birthday party. Many of our family members and friends asked for the recipe.

1 jar (24 ounces) salsa
1 can (15 ounces) chili with beans
2 cans (2-1/4 ounces *each*) sliced ripe olives, drained
12 ounces process cheese (Velveeta), cubed
Tortilla chips

In a small slow cooker, combine the salsa, chili and olives. Stir in cheese. Cover and cook on low for 1-2 hours or until the cheese is melted, stirring halfway through. Serve with tortilla chips. **Yield:** about 2 cups.

Slow-Cooked Salsa

Paddy's Reuben Dip

PADDY'S REUBEN DIP

Cook Time: 2 Hours

4 packages (2-1/2 ounces *each*) deli corned beef, finely chopped
1 package (8 ounces) cream cheese, cubed
1 can (8 ounces) sauerkraut, rinsed and drained
1 cup (8 ounces) sour cream
1 cup (4 ounces) shredded Swiss cheese
Rye bread *or* crackers

In a mini slow cooker, combine the first five ingredients. Cover and cook on low for 2 hours or until cheese is melted; stir until blended. Serve warm with bread or crackers. **Yield:** about 4 cups.

Mary Jane Kimmes
Hastings, Minnesota
This slow-cooked spread tastes just like a Reuben sandwich. Even when I double the recipe, I end up with an empty dish.

PIZZA SPREAD

Serve in Slow Cooker

1 pound ground beef
1 jar (26 ounces) marinara *or* spaghetti sauce
1 teaspoon dried oregano
4 cups (16 ounces) shredded mozzarella cheese
1 loaf Italian *or* French bread, cubed *or* sliced

In a saucepan, cook beef over medium heat until no longer pink; drain. Stir in marinara sauce and oregano. Gradually stir in cheese until melted.

Pour into a small slow cooker; cover and keep warm on low. Serve with bread. **Yield:** 8-10 servings.

Beverly Mons
Middletown, New York
For a satisfying snack, spread slices of Italian or French bread with this thick cheesy mixture. It's a very adaptable recipe that suits every occasion. It would also be good with Italian sausage instead of ground beef. Kids and adults love it.

CHAMPIONSHIP BEAN DIP

Cook Time: 2 Hours

Wendi Wavrin Law
Omaha, Nebraska
My friends and neighbors expect me to bring this irresistible dip to every gathering. When I arrive, they ask, "You brought your bean dip, didn't you?" If there are any leftovers, we use them to make bean and cheese burritos the next day.

1 can (16 ounces) refried beans
1 cup picante sauce
1 cup (4 ounces) shredded Monterey Jack cheese
1 cup (4 ounces) shredded cheddar cheese
3/4 cup sour cream
1 package (3 ounces) cream cheese, softened
1 tablespoon chili powder
1/4 teaspoon ground cumin
Tortilla chips and salsa

In a bowl, combine the first eight ingredients; transfer to a slow cooker. Cover and cook on high for 2 hours or until heated through, stirring once or twice. Serve with tortilla chips and salsa. **Yield:** 4-1/2 cups.

ALL-DAY MEATBALLS

Cook Time: 6 to 8 Hours

Cathy Ryan
Red Wing, Minnesota
For those who love to entertain but don't want last-minute fuss, these hearty meatballs are perfect. They're tender and have a tangy sauce.

1 cup milk
3/4 cup quick-cooking oats
3 tablespoons finely chopped onion
1-1/2 teaspoons salt
1-1/2 pounds ground beef
1 cup ketchup
1/2 cup water
3 tablespoons vinegar
2 tablespoons sugar

In a bowl, combine the first four ingredients. Crumble beef over the mixture and mix well. Shape into 1-in. balls. Place in a slow cooker.

In a bowl, combine the ketchup, water, vinegar and sugar; mix well. Pour over meatballs. Cover and cook on low for 6-8 hours or until the meat is no longer pink. **Yield:** 6 servings.

Championship Bean Dip

CHEDDAR FONDUE

Serve in Slow Cooker

Norene Wright
Manilla, Indiana
This cheesy blend, sparked with mustard and Worcestershire sauce, is yummy to snack on.

1/4 cup butter
1/4 cup all-purpose flour
1/2 teaspoon salt, optional
1/4 teaspoon pepper
1/4 teaspoon ground mustard
1/4 teaspoon Worcestershire
  sauce
1-1/2 cups milk
  2 cups (8 ounces) shredded
    cheddar cheese
Bread cubes, ham cubes, bite-size
  sausage *and/or* broccoli florets

In a saucepan, melt butter; stir in flour, salt if desired, pepper, mustard and Worcestershire sauce until smooth. Gradually add milk. Bring to a boil; cook and stir for 2 minutes or until thickened. Reduce heat. Add the cheese; cook and stir until melted.

Transfer to a slow cooker; cover and keep warm on low. Serve with bread, ham, sausage and/or broccoli. **Yield:** 2-1/2 cups.

PARTY SAUSAGES

Cook Time: 1 to 2 Hours

Jo Ann Renner
Xenia, Ohio
Don't want any leftovers on January 2? Serve these sausages January 1. I've never had even one end up uneaten. They're so tasty and not tricky to prepare.

2 pounds fully cooked smoked
  sausage links
1 bottle (8 ounces) Catalina
  salad dressing
1 bottle (8 ounces) Russian salad
  dressing
1/2 cup packed brown sugar
1/2 cup pineapple juice

Cut sausages diagonally into 1/2-in. slices; cook in a skillet over medium heat until lightly browned. Transfer sausages to a slow cooker; discard drippings.

Add dressings, sugar and juice to skillet; cook and stir over medium-low heat until sugar is dissolved. Pour over sausages. Cook on low for 1-2 hours or until heated through. Serve hot. **Yield:** 16 servings.

Editor's Note: French salad dressing may be substituted for one or both of the dressings.

Cheddar Fondue

TROUT CHOWDER

Cook Time: 1-1/2 to 2 Hours

1 medium onion, chopped
1 tablespoon butter
2 cups milk
1 cup ranch salad dressing
1 pound boneless trout fillets, skin removed
1 package (10 ounces) frozen broccoli cuts, thawed
1 cup cubed *or* shredded cheddar cheese
1 cup cubed *or* shredded Monterey Jack cheese

1/4 teaspoon garlic powder
Paprika, optional

In a skillet, saute onion in butter until tender. Transfer to a slow cooker; add milk, dressing, fish, broccoli, cheeses and garlic powder.

Cover and cook on high for 1-1/2 to 2 hours or until soup is bubbly and fish flakes easily with a fork. Sprinkle with paprika if desired. **Yield:** 6 servings.

Linda Kesselring
Corning, New York
This hearty chowder cooks conveniently in a slow cooker, so I can spend more time fishing and less in the kitchen. Broccoli adds fresh taste and lively color to the rich cheesy broth.

MEATY TOMATO SOUP

Cook Time: 8 Hours

1 can (28 ounces) diced tomatoes, undrained
2 cans (8 ounces *each*) tomato sauce
2 cups water
1/2 pound ground beef, cooked and drained
1/2 pound bulk pork sausage, cooked and drained
2 tablespoons dried minced onion
2 chicken bouillon cubes

3/4 teaspoon garlic salt
3/4 cup uncooked elbow macaroni
Shredded cheddar cheese, optional

In a slow cooker, combine the first eight ingredients; mix well. Cover and cook on low for 8 hours. Add macaroni and mix well.

Cover and cook 15 minutes longer or until macaroni is tender. Garnish with cheese if desired. **Yield:** 8-10 servings (2-1/4 quarts).

Ann Bost
Elkhart, Texas
As an elementary school librarian and church choir director, I've come to rely on and thoroughly enjoy slow-cooked meals. A sorority sister shared this recipe with me.

RICH FRENCH ONION SOUP

Cook Time: 5 to 7 Hours

Linda Adolph
Edmonton, Alberta
When entertaining guests, I bring out this tried-and-true soup while we're waiting for the main course. It's simple to make—just saute the onions early in the day and let the soup simmer until dinnertime.

6 large onions, chopped
1/2 cup butter
6 cans (10-1/2 ounces *each*) condensed beef broth, undiluted
1-1/2 teaspoons Worcestershire sauce
3 bay leaves
10 slices French bread, toasted
Shredded Parmesan and mozzarella cheeses

In a large skillet, saute onions in butter until crisp-tender. Transfer to an ungreased 5-qt. slow cooker. Add the broth, Worcestershire sauce and bay leaves.

Cover and cook on low for 5-7 hours or until the onions are tender. Discard bay leaves. Top each serving with French bread and cheeses. **Yield:** 10 servings.

SEAFOOD CHOWDER

Cook Time: 4 to 5 Hours

Marlene Muckenhirn
Delano, Minnesota
Our family requests this creamy chowder for Christmas Eve supper. It's an easy-to-serve and easy-to-clean-up meal between the church service and our gift exchange.

1 can (10-3/4 ounces) condensed cream of potato soup, undiluted
1 can (10-3/4 ounces) condensed cream of mushroom soup, undiluted
2-1/2 cups milk
4 medium carrots, finely chopped
2 medium potatoes, peeled and cut into 1/4-inch cubes
1 large onion, finely chopped
2 celery ribs, finely chopped
1 can (6-1/2 ounces) chopped clams, drained
1 can (6 ounces) medium shrimp, drained
4 ounces imitation crabmeat, flaked
5 bacon strips, cooked, crumbled

In a slow cooker, combine soups and milk. Stir in the vegetables. Cover and cook on low for 4-5 hours. Stir in clams, shrimp and crab; cover and heat through, about 20 minutes. Garnish each serving with bacon. **Yield:** 8 servings.

Rich French Onion Soup

FLAVORFUL WHITE CHILI

Cook Time: 8 to 9 Hours

Wilda Bensenhaver
Deland, Florida
For a tasty twist on conventional chili, try this low-fat version. It's packed with plenty of beans, tender grilled chicken and a zippy blend of spices.

1 pound dried great northern beans, rinsed and sorted
4 cups chicken broth
2 cups chopped onions
3 garlic cloves, minced
2 teaspoons ground cumin
1-1/2 teaspoons dried oregano
1 teaspoon ground coriander
1/8 teaspoon ground cloves
1/8 teaspoon cayenne pepper
1 can (4 ounces) chopped green chilies
1/2 pound boneless skinless chicken breast, grilled and cubed
1 teaspoon salt
3/4 cup shredded reduced-fat Mexican cheese blend

Place beans in a soup kettle or Dutch oven; add water to cover by 2 in. Bring to a boil; boil for 2 minutes. Remove from the heat; cover and let stand for 1 hour. Drain and rinse beans, discarding liquid.

Place beans in a slow cooker. Add the broth, onions, garlic and seasonings. Cover and cook on low for 7-8 hours or until beans are almost tender. Add the chilies, chicken and salt; cover and cook for 1 hour or until the beans are tender. Serve with cheese. **Yield:** 6 servings.

Faster Slow Cooking

To speed up cooking time on most slow cooker recipes, including soups and stews, follow the general rule that 1 hour on high is equal to 2 hours on low.

Flavorful White Chili

Slow Cooker Vegetable Soup

SLOW COOKER VEGETABLE SOUP

Cook Time: 8 Hours

1 pound boneless round steak, cut into 1/2-inch cubes
1 can (14-1/2 ounces) diced tomatoes, undrained
3 cups water
2 medium potatoes, peeled and cubed
2 medium onions, diced
3 celery ribs, sliced
2 carrots, sliced
3 beef bouillon cubes
1/2 teaspoon dried basil
1/2 teaspoon dried oregano
1/2 teaspoon salt
1/4 teaspoon pepper
1-1/2 cups frozen mixed vegetables

In a slow cooker, combine the first 12 ingredients. Cover and cook on high for 6 hours. Add vegetables; cover and cook on high 2 hours longer or until the meat and vegetables are tender. **Yield:** 8-10 servings (about 2-1/2 quarts).

Heather Thurmeier Pense, Saskatchewan
What a treat it is to come home from work and have this satisfying soup simmering away. It's a nice traditional beef soup with old-fashioned goodness. We pair it with fresh crusty rolls topped with melted mozzarella cheese.

SUMMER'S BOUNTY SOUP

Cook Time: 7 to 8 Hours

4 medium tomatoes, chopped
2 medium potatoes, peeled and cubed
2 cups halved fresh green beans
2 small zucchini, cubed
1 medium yellow summer squash, cubed
4 small carrots, thinly sliced
2 celery ribs, thinly sliced
1 cup cubed peeled eggplant
1 cup sliced fresh mushrooms
1 small onion, chopped
1 tablespoon minced fresh parsley
1 tablespoon salt-free garlic and herb seasoning
4 cups V8 juice

Combine all ingredients in a 5-qt. slow cooker. Cover and cook on low for 7-8 hours or until the vegetables are tender. **Yield:** 12-14 servings (about 3-1/2 quarts).

Victoria Zmarzley-Hahn Northampton, Pennsylvania
Lots of wonderfully fresh-tasting vegetables are showcased in this chunky soup. It's a great way to use up summer's excess produce. And it's so versatile—you can add or delete any vegetable to suit your taste.

Chili in Bread Bowls

Nancy Clancy
Standish, Maine
Some say you can have your cake and eat it, too...I say eat your chili and the bowl, too! I work the "graveyard shift" at the post office in Portland. During those hours, there is no place to buy meals, so I often bring in dishes like this.

1 tablespoon all-purpose flour
1/4 teaspoon salt
1/8 teaspoon pepper
1/2 pound *each* lean beef stew meat, boneless skinless chicken breast and boneless pork, cut into cubes
1 tablespoon vegetable oil
1 medium onion, chopped
1 medium green pepper, chopped
1 jalapeno pepper, seeded and chopped
1 can (28 ounces) diced tomatoes, drained
1 can (16 ounces) kidney beans, rinsed and drained
1 can (15-1/2 ounces) navy beans *or* great northern beans, rinsed and drained
1 can (8 ounces) tomato sauce
1 tablespoon chili powder
1 garlic clove, minced
1-1/2 teaspoons ground cumin
1/2 teaspoon dried basil
1/4 to 1/2 teaspoon cayenne pepper
9 large hard rolls
Sour cream, chopped green onions and sweet red pepper, optional

In a large resealable plastic bag, combine the flour, salt and pepper. Add meat in batches; toss to coat. In a large skillet, brown meat in oil in batches.

Transfer to a 5-qt. slow cooker with a slotted spoon. Stir in onion, peppers, tomatoes, beans, tomato sauce and seasonings. Cover and cook on low for 7-8 hours or until meat is tender.

Cut tops off rolls; carefully hollow out bottom halves. Spoon about 1 cup of chili into each roll. Garnish with sour cream, onions and red pepper if desired. **Yield:** 9 servings.

Editor's Note: When cutting or seeding hot peppers, use rubber or plastic gloves to protect your hands. Avoid touching your face.

Chili in Bread Bowls

Hearty Bean Soup

Hearty Bean Soup

Cook Time: 6 to 7 Hours

3 cups chopped parsnips
2 cups chopped carrots
1 cup chopped onion
1-1/2 cups dried great northern
 beans
5 cups water
1-1/2 pounds smoked ham hocks *or*
 ham shanks
2 garlic cloves, minced
2 teaspoons salt
1/2 teaspoon pepper
1/8 to 1/4 teaspoon hot pepper
 sauce

In a 5-qt. slow cooker, place parsnips, carrots and onion. Top with beans. Add water, ham, garlic, salt, pepper and hot pepper sauce. Cover and cook on high for 6-7 hours or until beans are tender.

Remove meat and bones when cool enough to handle. Cut meat into bite-size pieces and return to slow cooker; heat through. **Yield:** 6 servings.

Alice Schnoor
Arion, Iowa
This thick soup, with dried beans, ham and vegetables, is a tasty main dish or a satisfying first course.

Hominy Pork Soup

Cook Time: 4 Hours

1 pound pork chop suey meat,
 cut into 1/2-inch cubes
2 cans (15 ounces *each*) chili
 without beans
1 can (15-1/2 ounces) hominy,
 drained
1 can (8 ounces) tomato sauce
1 medium onion, chopped
1 bay leaf
1 tablespoon chili powder
1 teaspoon *each* dried basil,
 oregano and parsley flakes
1 teaspoon ground cumin
Warmed flour tortillas, shredded
 Monterey Jack cheese, sliced green
 onions and lime wedges, optional

In a slow cooker, combine the pork, chili, hominy, tomato sauce, onion and seasonings. Cover and cook on high for 4 hours or until meat is tender.

Discard bay leaf. Serve with tortillas, cheese, green onions and lime wedges if desired. **Yield:** 7 servings.

Raquel Walkup
San Pedro, California
Tender pork and hominy make this chili-like soup different from the usual offerings. It's an easy-to-prepare yet satisfying supper.

Potato Chowder

POTATO CHOWDER

Cook Time: 8 to 10 Hours

8 cups diced potatoes
1/3 cup chopped onion
3 cans (14-1/2 ounces *each*) chicken broth
1 can (10-3/4 ounces) condensed cream of chicken soup, undiluted
1/4 teaspoon pepper
1 package (8 ounces) cream cheese, cubed
1/2 pound sliced bacon, cooked and crumbled, optional
Snipped chives, optional

In a slow cooker, combine the first five ingredients. Cover and cook on low for 8-10 hours or until potatoes are tender. Add cream cheese; stir until blended. Garnish with bacon and chives if desired. **Yield:** 12 servings (3 quarts).

*Anna Mayer
Ft. Branch, Indiana
One of the ladies in our church quilting group brought this savory potato soup to a meeting. It's easy to assemble in the morning, then cook all day.*

HEARTY TOMATO PASTA SOUP

Cook Time: 3-1/2 to 4-1/2 Hours

1 pound bulk Italian sausage
6 cups beef broth
1 can (28 ounces) stewed tomatoes
1 can (15 ounces) tomato sauce
2 cups sliced zucchini
1 large onion, chopped
1 cup sliced carrots
1 cup sliced fresh mushrooms
1 medium green pepper, chopped
1/4 cup minced fresh parsley
2 teaspoons sugar
1 teaspoon dried oregano
1 teaspoon dried basil
1 garlic clove, minced
2 cups frozen cheese tortellini
Grated Parmesan cheese, optional

In a skillet, cook the sausage over medium heat until no longer pink; drain. Transfer to a 5-qt. slow cooker; add the next 13 ingredients. Cover and cook on high for 3-4 hours or until the vegetables are tender.

Cook tortellini according to package directions; drain. Stir into slow cooker; cover and cook 30 minutes longer. Serve with Parmesan cheese if desired. **Yield:** 14 servings (about 3-1/2 quarts).

*Lydia Kroese
Minnetonka, Minnesota
I adapted the original recipe for this satisfying soup so I could make it in the slow cooker. It's ideal for staff luncheons at the school where I work, since we don't have easy access to a stove or oven.*

TEXICAN CHILI

Cook Time: 9 to 10 Hours

Stacy Law
Cornish, Utah
This flavorful, meaty chili is my favorite…and it's so easy to prepare in the slow cooker. It's a great way to serve a crowd without last-minute preparation. I got the idea from my mother, who used her slow cooker often for soups and stews.

8 bacon strips, diced
2-1/2 pounds beef stew meat, cut into 1/2-inch cubes
2 cans (one 28 ounces, one 14-1/2 ounces) stewed tomatoes
2 cans (8 ounces *each*) tomato sauce
1 can (16 ounces) kidney beans, rinsed and drained
2 cups sliced carrots
1 medium onion, chopped
1 cup chopped celery
1/2 cup chopped green pepper
1/4 cup minced fresh parsley

1 tablespoon chili powder
1 teaspoon salt
1/2 teaspoon ground cumin
1/4 teaspoon pepper

In a skillet, cook bacon until crisp. Remove to paper towel to drain. Brown beef in the drippings over medium heat; drain.

Transfer to a 5-qt. slow cooker; add bacon and remaining ingredients. Cover and cook on low for 9-10 hours or until the meat is tender, stirring occasionally. **Yield:** 16-18 servings.

CURRIED LENTIL SOUP

Cook Time: 8 Hours

Christina Till
South Haven, Michigan
Curry gives a different taste sensation to this chili-like soup. It's delicious with a dollop of sour cream. My family welcomes it with open arms—and watering mouths.

4 cups hot water
1 can (28 ounces) crushed tomatoes
3 medium potatoes, peeled and diced
3 medium carrots, thinly sliced
1 large onion, chopped
1 celery rib, chopped
1 cup lentils
2 garlic cloves, minced

2 bay leaves
4 teaspoons curry powder
1-1/2 teaspoons salt

In a slow cooker, combine all ingredients; stir well. Cover and cook on low for 8 hours or until vegetables and lentils are tender. Discard the bay leaves before serving. **Yield:** 10 servings (2-1/2 quarts).

Texican Chili

Barbecued Beef Chili

Cook Time: 6 to 7 Hours

Phyllis Shyan
Elgin, Illinois
Served with bread and a side salad, this beefy chili makes a hearty meal. The recipe was inspired by two friends when we were talking about food at a potluck barbecue.

7 teaspoons chili powder
1 tablespoon garlic powder
2 teaspoons celery seed
1 teaspoon coarsely ground pepper
1/4 to 1/2 teaspoon cayenne pepper
1 fresh beef brisket (3 to 4 pounds)
1 medium green pepper, chopped
1 small onion, chopped
1 bottle (12 ounces) chili sauce
1 cup ketchup
1/2 cup barbecue sauce
1/3 cup packed brown sugar
1/4 cup cider vinegar
1/4 cup Worcestershire sauce
1 teaspoon ground mustard
1 can (15-1/2 ounces) hot chili beans
1 can (15-1/2 ounces) great northern beans, rinsed and drained

Combine the first five ingredients; rub over brisket. Cut into eight pieces; place in a slow cooker. Combine green pepper, onion, chili sauce, ketchup, barbecue sauce, brown sugar, vinegar, Worcestershire sauce and mustard; pour over meat. Cover and cook on high for 5-6 hours or until meat is tender.

Remove meat; cool slightly. Meanwhile, skim fat from cooking juices. Shred meat with two forks; return to slow cooker. Reduce heat to low. Stir in the beans. Cover and cook for 1 hour or until heated through. **Yield:** 12 servings.

Editor's Note: This recipe calls for a fresh beef brisket, not corned beef.

Barbecued Beef Chili

Beef 'n' Black Bean Soup

Beef 'n' Black Bean Soup

Cook Time: 6 to 7 Hours

1 pound ground beef
2 cans (14-1/2 ounces *each*) chicken broth
1 can (14-1/2 ounces) diced tomatoes, undrained
8 green onions, thinly sliced
3 medium carrots, thinly sliced
2 celery ribs, thinly sliced
2 garlic cloves, minced
1 tablespoon sugar
1-1/2 teaspoons dried basil
1/2 teaspoon salt
1/2 teaspoon dried oregano
1/2 teaspoon ground cumin
1/2 teaspoon chili powder
2 cans (15 ounces *each*) black beans, rinsed and drained
1-1/2 cups cooked rice

In a skillet over medium heat, cook beef until no longer pink; drain. Transfer to a slow cooker. Add the next 12 ingredients. Cover and cook on high for 1 hour.

Reduce heat to low; cook for 4-5 hours or until vegetables are tender. Add the beans and rice; cook 1 hour longer or until heated through. **Yield:** 10 servings (2-1/2 quarts).

Vickie Gibson
Gardendale, Alabama
I lead a busy life, so I'm always trying to come up with time-saving recipes. This zesty and colorful soup is one of my husband's favorites. It has been a hit at family gatherings, too.

Manhattan Clam Chowder

Cook Time: 8 to 10 Hours

3 celery ribs, sliced
1 large onion, chopped
1 can (14-1/2 ounces) sliced potatoes, drained
1 can (14-1/2 ounces) sliced carrots, drained
2 cans (6-1/2 ounces *each*) chopped clams
2 cups tomato juice
1-1/2 cups water
1/2 cup tomato puree
1 tablespoon dried parsley flakes
1-1/2 teaspoons dried thyme
1 teaspoon salt
1 bay leaf
2 whole black peppercorns

In a slow cooker, combine all ingredients; stir. Cover and cook on low for 8-10 hours or until the vegetables are tender. Remove bay leaf and peppercorns before serving. **Yield:** 9 servings.

Mary Dixon
Northville, Michigan
I came up with this delicious soup years ago when my husband and I both worked. It's easy to dump all the ingredients into the slow cooker in the morning…and great to come home to the aroma of dinner ready.

Savory Cheese Soup

SAVORY CHEESE SOUP

Cook Time: 7-1/2 to 8-1/2 Hours

3 cans (14-1/2 ounces *each*)
   chicken broth
1 small onion, chopped
1 large carrot, chopped
1 celery rib, chopped
1/4 cup chopped sweet red
   pepper
2 tablespoons butter
1 teaspoon salt
1/2 teaspoon pepper
1/3 cup all-purpose flour
1/3 cup cold water
1 package (8 ounces) cream
   cheese, cubed and softened
2 cups (8 ounces) shredded
   cheddar cheese
1 can (12 ounces) beer, optional

Optional toppings: croutons,
   popcorn, cooked crumbled bacon,
   sliced green onions

In a slow cooker, combine the first eight ingredients. Cover and cook on low for 7-8 hours. Combine flour and water until smooth; stir into soup.

Cover and cook on high 30 minutes longer or until soup is thickened. Stir in cream cheese and cheddar cheese until blended. Stir in beer if desired. Cover and cook on low until heated through. Serve with desired toppings. **Yield:** 6-8 servings.

Ann Huseby
Lakeville, Minnesota
This creamy soup is great at parties. Let guests serve themselves and choose from fun garnishes such as popcorn, croutons, green onions and bacon bits.

BUFFALO CHICKEN WING SOUP

Cook Time: 4 to 5 Hours

6 cups milk
3 cans (10-3/4 ounces *each*)
   condensed cream of chicken
   soup, undiluted
3 cups shredded cooked chicken
   (about 1 pound)
1 cup (8 ounces) sour cream
1/4 to 1/2 cup hot pepper sauce

Combine all ingredients in a slow cooker. Cover and cook on low for 4-5 hours. **Yield:** 8 servings (2 quarts).

Pat Farmer
Falconer, New York
Start with a small amount of hot sauce, then add more if needed to suit your family's tastes.

Slow-Cooked Chunky Chili

Slow-Cooked Chunky Chili

Cook Time: 4 to 5 Hours

1 pound ground beef
1 pound bulk pork sausage
4 cans (16 ounces *each*) kidney beans, rinsed and drained
2 cans (14-1/2 ounces *each*) diced tomatoes, undrained
2 cans (10 ounces *each*) diced tomatoes and green chilies, undrained
1 large onion, chopped
1 medium green pepper, chopped
1 envelope taco seasoning
1/2 teaspoon salt
1/4 teaspoon pepper

In a skillet, cook beef and sausage over medium heat until meat is no longer pink; drain. Transfer to a 5-qt. slow cooker. Stir in the remaining ingredients. Cover and cook on high for 4-5 hours or until the vegetables are tender. **Yield:** 3 quarts (12 servings).

Margie Shaw
Greenbrier, Arkansas
Pork sausage, ground beef and plenty of beans make this chili a hearty meal-starter. I serve bowls of it on cold days—or use it to fix chili dogs, tacos and more.

White Chili

Cook Time: 8 to 10 Hours

2 medium onions, chopped
4 garlic cloves, minced
2 quarts water
3 pounds chicken breasts *or* thighs, skin removed
1 pound dried navy beans
2 cans (4 ounces *each*) chopped green chilies
1 tablespoon ground cumin
2 teaspoons dried oregano
1 teaspoon salt
1/2 to 1 teaspoon cayenne pepper
1/2 teaspoon ground cloves
2 chicken bouillon cubes
Shredded Monterey Jack cheese
Sour cream
Dried chives and crushed red pepper flakes

Place the onions and garlic in a slow cooker. Add the next 10 ingredients; do not stir. Cook on high for 8-10 hours. Uncover and stir (the meat should fall off the bones). Remove bones. Stir to break up the meat. Spoon into bowls; top with cheese and sour cream if desired, and sprinkle with chives and pepper flakes. **Yield:** 12 servings (3 quarts).

Lana Rutledge
Shepherdsville, Kentucky
This savory white chili simmers all day on the kitchen countertop. When your hungry clan calls for dinner, you can ladle up steaming bowlfuls in a hurry. It's a wonderful alternative to traditional tomato-based chilies.

FRESH PUMPKIN SOUP

Cook Time: 8 to 10 Hours

*Jane Shapton
Portland, Oregon*
*This appealing soup
harvests the fall flavors
of just-picked pumpkins
and tart apples...and is
sure to warm you up on
a crisp autumn day.*

8 cups chopped fresh pumpkin
(about 3 pounds)
4 cups chicken broth
3 small tart apples, peeled and
chopped
1 medium onion, chopped
2 tablespoons lemon juice
2 tablespoons minced fresh
gingerroot
2 garlic cloves, minced
1/2 teaspoon salt
TOASTED PUMPKIN SEEDS:
1/2 cup pumpkin seeds
1 teaspoon canola oil
1/8 teaspoon salt

In a slow cooker, combine the first eight ingredients; mix well. Cover and cook on low for 8-10 hours or until pumpkin and apples are tender. Meanwhile, toss pumpkin seeds with oil and salt. Spread in an ungreased 15-in. x 10-in. x 1-in. baking pan. Bake at 250° for 50-60 minutes or until golden brown. Set aside.

Cool the pumpkin mixture slightly; process in batches in a blender or food processor. Transfer to a large saucepan; heat through. Garnish with toasted pumpkin seeds. **Yield:** 9 servings.

Broth or Bouillon?

Broth and bouillon are interchangeable. Broth is quicker, since it's ready to pour. However, one bouillon cube or 1 teaspoon of granules dissolved in 1 cup of boiling water may be substituted for 1 cup of broth in any recipe.

Fresh Pumpkin Soup

CORNY CHILI

Cook Time: 3 to 4 Hours

Marlene Olson
Hoople, North Dakota
This is so delicious and simple that I had to share it. I'm sure busy moms will be just as happy as I am with the taste and time-saving convenience of this pleasant chili.

1 pound ground beef
1 small onion, chopped
1 can (16 ounces) kidney beans, rinsed and drained
2 cans (14-1/2 ounces *each*) diced tomatoes, undrained
1 can (11 ounces) whole kernel corn, drained
3/4 cup picante sauce
1 tablespoon chili powder
1/4 to 1/2 teaspoon garlic powder
Corn chips, sour cream and shredded cheddar cheese, optional

In a skillet, cook beef and onion over medium heat until meat is no longer pink; drain. Transfer to a slow cooker. Stir in the beans, tomatoes, corn, picante sauce, chili powder and garlic powder.

Cover and cook on low for 3-4 hours or until heated through. Serve with corn chips, sour cream and cheese if desired. **Yield:** 4-6 servings.

HAMBURGER VEGETABLE SOUP

Cook Time: 8 to 9 Hours

Theresa Jackson
Cicero, New York
I work full time and have a family of four. We sit down to a home-cooked meal just about every night, many times thanks to my slow cooker. This soup is often on the menu.

1 pound ground beef
1 medium onion, chopped
2 garlic cloves, minced
4 cups V8 juice
1 can (14-1/2 ounces) stewed tomatoes
2 cups coleslaw mix
2 cups frozen green beans
2 cups frozen corn
2 tablespoons Worcestershire sauce
1 teaspoon dried basil
1/2 teaspoon salt
1/4 teaspoon pepper

In a saucepan, cook beef, onion and garlic over medium heat until meat is no longer pink; drain.

In a slow cooker, combine remaining ingredients. Stir in beef mixture. Cover and cook on low for 8-9 hours or until the vegetables are tender. **Yield:** 10 servings.

Corny Chili

Texas Black Bean Soup

TEXAS BLACK BEAN SOUP

Cook Time: 4 to 5 Hours

2 cans (15 ounces *each*) black
  beans, rinsed and drained
1 can (14-1/2 ounces) stewed
  tomatoes *or* Mexican stewed
  tomatoes, cut up
1 can (14-1/2 ounces) diced
  tomatoes *or* diced tomatoes
  with green chilies
1 can (14-1/2 ounces) chicken
  broth
1 can (11 ounces) Mexicorn,
  drained

2 cans (4 ounces *each*) chopped
  green chilies
4 green onions, thinly sliced
2 to 3 tablespoons chili powder
1 teaspoon ground cumin
1/2 teaspoon dried minced garlic

In a slow cooker, combine all ingredients.
Cover and cook on high for 4-5 hours or
until heated through. **Yield:** 8-10 servings
(about 2-1/2 quarts).

Pamela Scott
Garland, Texas
This hearty soup made
with convenient canned
items is perfect for
spicing up a family
gathering on a cool day.
It tastes great and
requires so little time
and attention.

SMOKED SAUSAGE SOUP

Cook Time: 5 to 8 Hours

2 cups chopped onion
2 tablespoons butter
2 cups cubed cooked chicken
1 pound cooked smoked
  sausage, cut into bite-size
  pieces
3 cups sliced celery
3 cups sliced summer squash
2 cups chicken broth
1-1/2 cups minced fresh parsley
1 can (8 ounces) tomato sauce
2 tablespoons cornstarch
2 tablespoons poultry seasoning

1 teaspoon dried oregano
1 teaspoon ground cumin
1 teaspoon Liquid Smoke,
  optional
1/2 teaspoon pepper

In a skillet or microwave, cook onion in
butter until softened. Transfer to a 3-qt.
or larger slow cooker. Add remaining ingredients, stirring to blend. Cook on high
for 5-8 hours. **Yield:** 6-8 servings (2-1/2
quarts).

Rachel Lyn Grasmick
Rocky Ford, Colorado
This rich soup is packed
with vegetables, sausage
and chicken. I guarantee
it's unlike any other
soup you've ever tasted.

Pork Chili

Pork Chili

Cook Time: 6 Hours

2-1/2 pounds boneless pork, cut
    into 1-inch cubes
2 tablespoons vegetable oil
1 can (28 ounces) diced
    tomatoes, undrained
1 can (15-1/2 ounces) chili
    beans, undrained
1 can (8 ounces) tomato sauce
1/4 cup salsa
1/4 cup chopped onion
1/4 cup chopped green pepper
1 tablespoon chili powder
1 teaspoon minced jalapeno
    pepper
1/4 teaspoon garlic powder
1/4 teaspoon cayenne pepper
1/4 teaspoon pepper
1/4 teaspoon salt

In a large skillet over medium-high heat, brown pork in oil; drain. Place in a slow cooker; add remaining ingredients. Cover and cook on high for 2 hours. Reduce heat to low and cook 4 hours longer.
Yield: 10-12 servings.

Editor's Note: When cutting or seeing hot peppers, use rubber or plastic gloves to protect your hands. Avoid touching your face.

Linda Temple
St. Joseph, Missouri
My husband usually tries to avoid spending time in the kitchen, but he'll frequently offer to prepare this easy chili. Of course, he always eagerly serves as taste tester!

Busy Day Beef Stew

(Also pictured on front cover)

Cook Time: 10 Hours

Beth Wyatt
Paris, Kentucky
I call this my "lazy" stew because it's so easy to make on busy days. It keeps folks coming back for more.

1 boneless beef chuck roast
(1 to 1-1/2 pounds)
1 envelope onion soup mix
2 teaspoons browning sauce, optional
1/2 teaspoon salt
1/2 teaspoon pepper
6 cups water
2 cups cubed peeled potatoes
(1/2-inch pieces)
6 to 8 medium carrots, cut into chunks
1 medium onion, chopped
1 cup frozen peas, thawed
1 cup frozen corn, thawed
5 tablespoons cornstarch
6 tablespoons cold water

Place roast in a slow cooker; sprinkle with soup mix, browning sauce if desired, salt and pepper. Pour water over meat. Cover and cook on low for 8 hours.

Remove roast to a cutting board; let stand for 5 minutes. Add vegetables to slow cooker. Cube beef and return to slow cooker. Cover and cook on low for 1-1/2 hours or until vegetables are tender. Combine cornstarch and cold water until smooth; stir into stew. Cover and cook on high for 30-45 minutes or until thickened. **Yield:** 8-10 servings.

Easy Warm Bread

To warm rolls or slices of bread to go with a stew, wrap them in foil and set them in the covered cooker right on top of the hot cooked stew as you're setting the table to serve.

Busy Day Beef Stew

MINESTRONE STEW

Cook Time: 4 to 6 Hours

Janie Hoskins
Red Bluff, California
This stew is made from convenient pantry ingredients, plus it's easy on the pocketbook. You're sure to like the taste.

1 pound ground beef
1 small onion, chopped
1 can (19 ounces) ready-to-serve minestrone soup
1 can (15 ounces) pinto beans, rinsed and drained
1 can (14-1/2 ounces) stewed tomatoes
1 can (11 ounces) whole kernel corn, drained
1 can (4 ounces) chopped green chilies

1 teaspoon salt
1/2 teaspoon garlic powder
1/2 teaspoon onion powder

In a skillet, cook beef and onion over medium heat until meat is no longer pink; drain. Transfer to a slow cooker. Add the remaining ingredients; mix well. Cover and cook on low for 4-6 hours or until heated through. **Yield:** 8 servings.

HEARTY PORK STEW

Cook Time: 8-1/2 Hours

Rebecca Overy
Evanston, Wyoming
Tender chunks of pork combine with colorful tomatoes and green peppers in this spicy, hearty stew. I garnish bowls of it with chopped hard-cooked eggs and green onions.

1-1/2 to 2 pounds boneless pork, cut into 1-inch cubes
4 cups water
1 can (14-1/2 ounces) stewed tomatoes
1 medium onion, chopped
1 medium green pepper, chopped
1/3 cup soy sauce
1 to 2 tablespoons chili powder
1 tablespoon dried celery flakes
1/2 teaspoon garlic powder

1/2 teaspoon pepper
1/3 cup cornstarch
1/3 cup cold water
Hot cooked noodles

In a slow cooker, combine the first 10 ingredients. Cover and cook on low for 8 hours. Combine cornstarch and water until smooth; gradually stir into slow cooker. Cover and cook on high for 30 minutes or until slightly thickened. Serve in bowls over noodles. **Yield:** 8-10 servings.

Minestrone Stew

Chicken Mushroom Stew

Cook Time: 4 Hours

*Kim Marie
Van Rheenen
Mendota, Illinois
As it simmers, the
flavors blend beautifully
in this pot of chicken,
vegetables and herbs.
This stew always draws
compliments from those
who try it.*

6 boneless skinless chicken
  breast halves (1-1/2 pounds)
2 tablespoons vegetable oil,
  divided
8 ounces fresh mushrooms,
  sliced
1 medium onion, diced
3 cups diced zucchini
1 cup diced green pepper
4 garlic cloves, minced
3 medium tomatoes, diced
1 can (6 ounces) tomato paste
3/4 cup water
2 teaspoons salt
1 teaspoon *each* dried thyme,
  oregano, marjoram and basil

Cut chicken into 1-in. cubes; brown in 1 tablespoon oil in a large skillet. Transfer to a slow cooker. In the same skillet, saute the mushrooms, onion, zucchini, green pepper and garlic in remaining oil until crisp-tender. Place in slow cooker.

Add tomatoes, tomato paste, water and seasonings. Cover and cook on low for 4 hours or until the vegetables are tender. **Yield:** 6 servings.

Chicken Mushroom Stew

Hobo Meatball Stew

Hobo Meatball Stew

Cook Time: 4 to 5 Hours

1 pound ground beef
1-1/2 teaspoons salt, *divided*
1/2 teaspoon pepper, *divided*
4 medium potatoes, peeled and cut into chunks
4 medium carrots, cut into chunks
1 large onion, cut into chunks
1/2 cup ketchup
1/2 cup water
1-1/2 teaspoons vinegar
1/2 teaspoon dried basil

In a bowl, combine beef, 1 teaspoon salt and 1/4 teaspoon pepper; mix well. Shape into 1-in. balls. In a skillet over medium heat, brown meatballs on all sides; drain. Place the potatoes, carrots and onion in a slow cooker; top with the meatballs.

Combine the ketchup, water, vinegar, basil, and remaining salt and pepper; pour over meatballs. Cover and cook on high for 4-5 hours or until the vegetables are tender. **Yield:** 4 servings.

Margery Bryan
Royal City, Washington
Basic ingredients make this hearty stew a favorite. I usually have everything on hand for this recipe, so it's simple to load up the slow cooker at noon. When I get home, dinner's ready.

Green Chili Stew

Cook Time: 7 to 8 Hours

2 pounds beef stew meat, cut into 1-inch cubes
2 medium onions, chopped
2 tablespoons vegetable oil
1 can (15 ounces) pinto beans, rinsed and drained
1 can (14-1/2 ounces) diced tomatoes, undrained
2 cans (4 ounces *each*) chopped green chilies
1 cup water
3 beef bouillon cubes
1 garlic clove, minced
1 teaspoon sugar
1/2 teaspoon salt
1/4 teaspoon pepper
Shredded cheddar *or* Monterey Jack cheese, optional

In a skillet, brown beef and onions in oil; drain. Transfer to a 5-qt. slow cooker. Combine beans, tomatoes, chilies, water, bouillon, garlic, sugar, salt and pepper; pour over beef. Cover; cook on low for 7-8 hours or until beef is tender. Sprinkle with cheese if desired. **Yield:** 8 servings.

Jacqueline Thompson
Graves
Lawrenceville, Georgia
This stew is much heartier than most—and very tasty, too. My family especially enjoys the zippy broth and the generous amounts of tender beef. They frequently request second helpings.

Beef Barley Stew

Cook Time: 6 to 7 Hours

Barb Smith
Regina, Saskatchewan
On cool days, which we get plenty of here, I like to get out my slow cooker and make up a batch of this comforting stew. Trying to appeal to 10 picky eaters in our large household is not too easy, but with this recipe, everyone digs right in.

1-1/2 pounds beef stew meat, cut into 1-inch pieces
1 medium onion, chopped
2 tablespoons vegetable oil
1 quart water
1 can (15 ounces) tomato sauce
5 medium carrots, cut into 1/2-inch pieces
1 celery rib, thinly sliced
2 teaspoons salt
1/2 teaspoon dried oregano
1/2 teaspoon paprika
1/4 teaspoon pepper
2 cups fresh *or* frozen green beans
2 cups fresh *or* frozen corn
3/4 cup medium pearl barley

In a skillet, brown beef and onion in oil; drain. Transfer to a 5-qt. slow cooker. Add water, tomato sauce, carrots, celery, salt, oregano, paprika and pepper.

Cover and cook on low for 4-5 hours. Add beans, corn and barley; cover and cook on low 2 hours longer or until barley, beef and vegetables are tender. **Yield:** 6-8 servings.

Beef Barley Stew

CHICKEN STEW OVER BISCUITS

Cook Time: 8 to 9 Hours

Kathy Garrett
Browns Mills,
New Jersey
A pleasant sauce coats
this chicken and veggie
dinner that's slow-
cooked to tender
perfection, then served
over biscuits.

2 envelopes chicken gravy mix
2 cups water
3/4 cup white wine *or* chicken
  broth
2 garlic cloves, minced
1 tablespoon minced fresh
  parsley
1 to 2 teaspoons chicken
  bouillon granules
1/2 teaspoon pepper
5 medium carrots, cut
  into 1-inch chunks
1 large onion, cut into eight
  wedges
1 broiler/fryer chicken
  (3 to 4 pounds), cut up
3 tablespoons all-purpose flour
1/3 cup cold water
1 tube (7-1/2 ounces)
  refrigerated buttermilk
  biscuits

In a slow cooker, combine gravy mix, water, wine or broth, garlic, parsley, bouillon and pepper until blended. Add the carrots, onion and chicken. Cover and cook on low for 7-8 hours. Increase heat to high.

In a small bowl, combine the flour and cold water until smooth; gradually stir into slow cooker. Cover and cook for 1 hour. Meanwhile, bake biscuits according to package directions. Place biscuits in soup bowls; top with stew. **Yield:** 4-6 servings.

SAVORY SANDWICHES

CHAPTER 3

Fiesta Pork Sandwiches

Fiesta Pork Sandwiches

Cook Time: 8 to 10 Hours

1 boneless pork shoulder roast
   (3 to 4 pounds)
1/3 cup lime juice
2 tablespoons grapefruit juice
2 tablespoons water
1 bay leaf
6 garlic cloves, minced
1/2 teaspoon salt
1/2 teaspoon dried oregano
1/2 teaspoon chili powder
2 tablespoons olive oil
1 large onion, thinly sliced
12 to 14 sandwich rolls, split

Cut the roast in half; pierce several times with a fork. Place in a large resealable plastic bag or shallow glass container. Combine the next eight ingredients; pour over roast. Cover and refrigerate overnight, turning occasionally.

Drain, reserving marinade. In a skillet over medium heat, brown the roast in oil on all sides. Place onion, roast and marinade in a slow cooker. Cover and cook on high for 2 hours.

Reduce heat to low; cook 6-8 hours longer or until the meat is tender. Remove roast; shred or thinly slice. Discard the bay leaf. Skim fat from cooking juices and transfer to a saucepan; bring to a rolling boil. Serve pork on rolls with juices as a dipping sauce. **Yield:** 12-14 servings.

Yvette Massey
La Luz, New Mexico
This is an easy and flavorful dish that my family really enjoys. When I make these sandwiches for company, I usually prepare the meat the day before, so I can concentrate on side dishes and relaxing with my friends.

How to Shred Meat

For the best results when shredding meat, follow this method:

Remove the cooked meat from the slow cooker, with a slotted spoon if necessary. Reserve the cooking liquid if called for. Place the meat in a shallow pan or platter. With two forks, pull the meat into thin shreds. Return the shredded meat to the slow cooker to warm or use as the recipe directs.

SAVORY BEEF SANDWICHES

Cook Time: 6 to 8 Hours

Lynn Williamson
Hayward, Wisconsin
Before heading to work in the morning, I'll get this going in the slow cooker. Then it's all ready to serve as soon as my husband and I walk in.

1 tablespoon dried minced onion
2 teaspoons salt
2 teaspoons garlic powder
2 teaspoons dried oregano
1 teaspoon dried rosemary, crushed
1 teaspoon caraway seeds
1 teaspoon dried marjoram
1 teaspoon celery seed
1/4 teaspoon cayenne pepper
1 boneless chuck roast (3 to 4 pounds), halved
8 to 10 sandwich rolls, split

Combine seasonings; rub over roast. Place in a slow cooker. Cover and cook on low for 6-8 hours or until meat is tender. Shred with a fork. Serve on rolls. **Yield:** 8-10 servings.

Editor's Note: No liquid is added to the slow cooker. The moisture comes from the roast.

ITALIAN BEEF HOAGIES

Cook Time: 8 Hours

Lori Piatt
Danville, Illinois
You'll need just five ingredients to feed a crowd these tender tangy sandwiches. On weekends, I start the roast the night before, so I can shred it in the morning.

1 boneless sirloin tip roast (about 4 pounds), halved
2 envelopes Italian salad dressing mix
2 cups water
1 jar (16 ounces) mild pepper rings, undrained
18 hoagie buns, split

Place roast in a 5-qt. slow cooker. Combine the salad dressing mix and water; pour over roast. Cover and cook on low for 8 hours or until meat is tender.

Remove meat; shred with a fork and return to slow cooker. Add pepper rings; heat through. Spoon 1/2 cup meat mixture onto each bun. **Yield:** 18 servings.

Savory Beef Sandwiches

HERBED FRENCH DIP SANDWICHES

Cook Time: 10 to 12 Hours

Dianne Joy Richardson
Colorado Springs,
Colorado
I found this recipe in one of our local publications. It's great for an easy meal any time of year, since the meat cooks all day without any attention.

1 lean beef roast (3 to 4 pounds)
1/2 cup soy sauce
1 beef bouillon cube
1 bay leaf
3 to 4 whole peppercorns
1 teaspoon dried rosemary, crushed
1 teaspoon dried thyme
1 teaspoon garlic powder
Hard rolls *or* French bread

Remove and discard all visible fat from roast. Place in a slow cooker. Combine soy sauce, bouillon and spices; pour over roast. Add water to almost cover roast. Cover and cook over low heat for 10-12 hours or until meat is very tender.

Remove meat and discard bay leaf; reserve cooking juices. Shred meat with two forks. Serve on hard rolls or French bread slices. Serve cooking juices as a dipping sauce. **Yield:** 12 servings.

DILLY BEEF SANDWICHES

Cook Time: 8 to 9 Hours

Donna Blankenheim
Madison, Wisconsin
My sister shared this recipe, which puts a twist on the traditional barbecue sandwich. As a mother of four, she never has much time to cook, but she does like to entertain. This crowd-pleaser, which takes mere minutes to prep, is perfect for our large family gatherings.

1 boneless beef chuck roast (3 to 4 pounds)
1 jar (16 ounces) whole dill pickles, undrained
1/2 cup chili sauce
2 garlic cloves, minced
10 to 12 hamburger buns, split

Cut roast in half and place in a slow cooker. Add pickles with juice, chili sauce and garlic. Cover and cook on low for 8-9 hours or until beef is tender.

Discard pickles. Remove roast. When cool enough to handle, shred the meat. Return to the sauce and heat through. Using a slotted spoon, fill each bun with about 1/2 cup meat mixture. **Yield:** 10-12 servings.

Herbed French Dip Sandwiches

Hearty New England Dinner

Cook Time: 7-1/2 to 9-1/2 Hours

2 medium carrots, sliced
1 medium onion, sliced
1 celery rib, sliced
1 boneless chuck roast
  (about 3 pounds)
1 teaspoon salt, *divided*
1/4 teaspoon pepper
1 envelope onion soup mix
2 cups water
1 tablespoon vinegar
1 bay leaf
1/2 small head cabbage, cut into
  wedges
3 tablespoons butter
2 tablespoons all-purpose flour
1 tablespoon dried minced
  onion
2 tablespoons prepared
  horseradish

Place carrots, onion and celery in a 5-qt. slow cooker. Place the roast on top; sprinkle with 1/2 teaspoon salt and pepper. Add soup mix, water, vinegar and bay leaf. Cover and cook on low for 7-9 hours or until beef is tender.

Remove beef and keep warm; discard bay leaf. Add cabbage. Cover and cook on high for 30-40 minutes or until cabbage is tender.

Meanwhile, melt butter in a small saucepan; stir in flour and onion. Add 1-1/2 cups cooking liquid from the slow cooker. Stir in horseradish and remaining salt; bring to a boil.

Cook and stir over low heat until thick and smooth, about 2 minutes. Serve with roast and vegetables. **Yield:** 6-8 servings.

Claire McCombs
San Diego, California
This favorite slow-cooker recipe came from a friend. At first, my husband was a bit skeptical about a roast that wasn't fixed in the oven, but he loves the old-fashioned goodness of this version. The horseradish in the gravy adds zip.

Try to Trim Down

When preparing meat or poultry for the slow cooker, trim off excess fat. It retains heat, and large amounts of fat could raise the temperature of the cooking liquid, causing the meat to overcook.

Slow-Cooked Tamale Casserole

RIVAL® CROCK·POT® STONEWARE SLOW COOKER

High

SLOW-COOKED TAMALE CASSEROLE

Cook Time: 4 Hours

1 pound ground beef
1 egg
1-1/2 cups milk
3/4 cup cornmeal
1 can (15-1/4 ounces) whole kernel corn, drained
1 can (14-1/2 ounces) diced tomatoes, undrained
1 can (2-1/4 ounces) sliced ripe olives, drained
1 envelope chili seasoning
1 teaspoon seasoned salt
1 cup (4 ounces) shredded cheddar cheese

In a skillet, cook beef over medium heat until no longer pink; drain. In a bowl, combine the egg, milk and cornmeal until smooth. Add corn, tomatoes, olives, chili seasoning, seasoned salt and beef. Transfer to a greased slow cooker.

Cover and cook on high for 3 hours and 45 minutes. Sprinkle with cheese; cover and cook 15 minutes longer or until cheese is melted. **Yield:** 6 servings.

*Diana Briggs
Veneta, Oregon
I've been making this recipe for years because my family really likes it. It's great for busy days, since you assemble it earlier in the day and let it cook.*

SMOKY BEEF 'N' BEANS

Cook Time: 6 to 7 Hours

1 pound ground beef
1 cup chopped onion
12 bacon strips, cooked and crumbled
2 cans (16 ounces *each*) pork and beans
1 can (16 ounces) kidney beans, rinsed and drained
1 can (16 ounces) butter beans, drained
1 cup ketchup
1/4 cup packed brown sugar
3 tablespoons vinegar
1/2 teaspoon salt
1/4 teaspoon pepper
1 teaspoon Liquid Smoke, optional

In a skillet over medium heat, cook the beef and onion until meat is no longer pink; drain. Transfer to a slow cooker. Stir in the next nine ingredients. Add Liquid Smoke if desired. Cover and cook on low for 6-7 hours or until heated through. **Yield:** 8 servings.

*Anita Curtis
Camarillo, California
Liquid Smoke gives a unique taste to this thick and hearty combination of beef and beans. I serve it with a crisp salad to make a complete meal.*

Slow-Cooked Swiss Steak

Slow-Cooked Swiss Steak

Cook Time: 8 to 9 Hours

3/4 cup all-purpose flour
1 teaspoon pepper
1/4 teaspoon salt
2 to 2-1/2 pounds boneless
  round steak
1 to 2 tablespoons butter
1 can (10-3/4 ounces) condensed
  cream of mushroom soup,
  undiluted
1-1/3 cups water
1 cup sliced celery, optional
1/2 cup chopped onion
1 garlic clove, minced
1 to 3 teaspoons beef bouillon
  granules

In a shallow bowl, combine flour, pepper and salt. Cut steak into six serving-size pieces; dredge in flour mixture. In a skillet, brown steak in butter. Transfer to a slow cooker. Combine the remaining ingredients; pour over steak. Cover and cook on low for 8-9 hours or until the meat is tender. **Yield:** 6 servings.

Kathie Morris
Redmond, Oregon
Everyone raves about how tender and rich-tasting this dish is. Leftovers from a double batch make super Stroganoff the next night. I crumble the meat and mix it with the gravy, plus sour cream and Worcestershire sauce.

Flank Steak Roll-Up

Cook Time: 8 to 10 Hours

1 can (4 ounces) mushroom
  stems and pieces, undrained
2 tablespoons butter, melted
1 package (6 ounces) seasoned
  stuffing mix
1 beef flank steak (1-3/4 pounds)
1 envelope brown gravy mix
1/4 cup chopped green onions
1/4 cup dry red wine *or beef broth*

In a bowl, toss the mushrooms, butter and dry stuffing mix. Spread over steak to within 1 in. of edges. Roll up jelly-roll style, starting with a long side; tie with kitchen string. Place in a slow cooker. Prepare gravy mix according to package directions; add onions and wine or broth. Pour over meat. Cover and cook on low for 8-10 hours.

Remove meat to a serving platter and keep warm. Strain cooking juices and thicken if desired. Remove string from roll-up; slice and serve with gravy. **Yield:** 6 servings.

Sheryl Johnson
Las Vegas, Nevada
As a working mother of five hungry boys, I rely on my slow cooker to give me a head start on meals. For this special yet filling dish, I roll stuffing mix and mushrooms into flank steak before simmering it in an easy gravy.

Slow-Cooked Pepper Steak

Cook Time: 6 to 7 Hours

Sue Gronholz
Columbus, Wisconsin
After a long day in our greenhouse raising bedding plants for sale, I appreciate coming in to this hearty beef dish for supper.

1-1/2 to 2 pounds beef round steak
2 tablespoons vegetable oil
1/4 cup soy sauce
1 cup chopped onion
1 garlic clove, minced
1 teaspoon sugar
1/2 teaspoon salt
1/4 teaspoon pepper
1/4 teaspoon ground ginger
4 tomatoes, cut into eighths
   or 1 can (14-1/2 ounces) diced tomatoes, undrained
2 large green peppers, cut into strips
1/2 cup cold water
1 tablespoon cornstarch
Hot cooked noodles *or* rice

Cut beef into 3-in. x 1-in. strips; brown in oil in a skillet. Transfer to a slow cooker. Combine the next seven ingredients; pour over beef. Cover and cook on low for 5-6 hours or until meat is tender. Add tomatoes and green peppers; cook on low for 1 hour longer. Combine the cold water and cornstarch to make a paste; stir into liquid in slow cooker and cook on high until thickened. Serve over noodles or rice. **Yield:** 6-8 servings.

Saucy Italian Roast

Cook Time: 8 to 9 Hours

Jan Roat
Grass Range, Montana
This tender roast is one of my favorite fix-it-and-forget-it meals. I thicken the juices with a little flour and add ketchup, then serve the sauce and beef slices over pasta. It's deliciously different.

1 boneless rump roast (3 to 3-1/2 pounds)
1/2 to 1 teaspoon salt
1/2 teaspoon garlic powder
1/4 teaspoon pepper
1 jar (4-1/2 ounces) sliced mushrooms, drained
1 medium onion, diced
1 jar (14 ounces) spaghetti sauce
1/4 to 1/2 cup red wine *or* beef broth
Hot cooked pasta

Cut the roast in half. Combine salt, garlic powder and pepper; rub over roast. Place in a 5-qt. slow cooker. Top with mushrooms and onion. Combine the spaghetti sauce and wine or broth; pour over meat and vegetables. Cover and cook on low for 8-9 hours or until meat is tender. Slice roast; serve over pasta with pan juices. **Yield:** 8-10 servings.

Slow-Cooked Pepper Steak

Slow-Cooked Rump Roast

SLOW-COOKED RUMP ROAST

Cook Time: 10-1/2 to 11-1/2 Hours

1 boneless beef rump roast
　(3 to 3-1/2 pounds)
2 tablespoons vegetable oil
4 medium carrots, halved
　lengthwise and cut into 2-inch
　pieces
3 medium potatoes, peeled and
　cut into chunks
2 small onions, sliced
1/2 cup water
6 to 8 tablespoons horseradish
1/4 cup red wine vinegar
1/4 cup Worcestershire sauce
2 garlic cloves, minced
1-1/2 to 2 teaspoons celery salt
3 tablespoons cornstarch
1/3 cup cold water

Cut roast in half. In a large skillet, brown meat on all sides in oil over medium-high heat; drain. Place carrots and potatoes in a 5-qt. slow cooker. Top with meat and onions. Combine the water, horseradish, vinegar, Worcestershire sauce, garlic and celery salt. Pour over meat. Cover and cook on low for 10-11 hours or until meat and vegetables are tender.

Combine cornstarch and cold water until smooth; stir into slow cooker. Cover and cook on high for 30 minutes or until gravy is thickened. **Yield:** 6-8 servings.

Mimi Walker
Palmyra, Pennsylvania
Cooking pot roast in horseradish sauce in the slow cooker is a tasty new twist. It gives a tangy flavor, tender vegetables and great gravy that even young kids enjoy.

Spread It Out

For meats to cook evenly in the slow cooker, allow some space between the pieces, so the heat can circulate and the seasonings can be nicely distributed.

Slow-Cooked Meat Loaf

Cook Time: 8 to 9 Hours

Marna Heitz
Farley, Iowa
What could be more comforting to come home to than moist and tender homemade meat loaf? This one retains its shape in the slow cooker and slices beautifully. Because the vegetables cook with the meat, the entire dinner is ready at the same time.

1 egg
1/4 cup milk
2 slices day-old bread, cubed
1/4 cup finely chopped onion
2 tablespoons finely chopped green pepper
1 teaspoon salt
1/4 teaspoon pepper
1-1/2 pounds lean ground beef
1/4 cup ketchup
8 medium carrots, cut into 1-inch chunks
8 small red potatoes

In a bowl, beat egg and milk. Stir in the bread cubes, onion, green pepper, salt and pepper. Add the beef and mix well. Shape into a round loaf. Place in a 5-qt. slow cooker. Spread ketchup on top of loaf. Arrange carrots around loaf. Peel a strip around the center of each potato; place potatoes over carrots.

Cover and cook on high for 1 hour. Reduce heat to low; cover and cook 7-8 hours longer or until meat is no longer pink and the vegetables are tender. **Yield:** 4 servings.

Beef and Beans

Cook Time: 6-1/2 to 8-1/2 Hours

Marie Leadmon
Bethesda, Maryland
This deliciously spicy steak and beans over rice will have family and friends asking for more. It's a favorite in my recipe collection because it's so simple and so good.

1-1/2 pounds boneless round steak
1 tablespoon prepared mustard
1 tablespoon chili powder
1/2 teaspoon salt
1/4 teaspoon pepper
1 garlic clove, minced
2 cans (14-1/2 ounces *each*) diced tomatoes, undrained
1 medium onion, chopped
1 beef bouillon cube, crushed
1 can (16 ounces) kidney beans, rinsed and drained
Hot cooked rice

Cut steak into thin strips. Combine mustard, chili powder, salt, pepper and garlic in a bowl; add steak and toss to coat. Transfer to a slow cooker; add tomatoes, onion and bouillon. Cover and cook on low for 6-8 hours. Stir in beans; cook 30 minutes longer. Serve over rice. **Yield:** 8 servings.

Slow-Cooked Meat Loaf

CHILI MAC

Cook Time: 6 Hours

Marie Posavec
Berwyn, Illinois
This recipe has appeared on my menus once a month for more than 40 years...it's never failed to please. I've also turned it into a soup by adding a can of beef broth.

1 pound ground beef, cooked and drained
2 cans (15 ounces *each*) hot chili beans, undrained
2 large green peppers, chopped
1 large onion, chopped
4 celery ribs, chopped
1 can (8 ounces) tomato sauce
1 envelope chili seasoning
2 garlic cloves, minced
1 package (7 ounces) elbow macaroni, cooked and drained
Salt and pepper to taste

In a slow cooker, combine the first eight ingredients; mix well. Cover and cook on low for 6 hours or until heated through. Stir in the macaroni; mix well. Season with salt and pepper. **Yield:** 12 servings.

SLOW-COOKED SHORT RIBS

Cook Time: 9 to 10 Hours

Pam Halfhill
Medina, Ohio
Smothered in a mouth-watering barbecue sauce, these meaty ribs are a popular entree wherever I serve them. The recipe is great for a busy cook—after everything is combined, the slow cooker does all the work.

2/3 cup all-purpose flour
2 teaspoons salt
1/2 teaspoon pepper
4 to 4-1/2 pounds boneless beef short ribs
1/4 to 1/3 cup butter
1 large onion, chopped
1-1/2 cups beef broth
3/4 cup red wine vinegar
3/4 cup packed brown sugar
1/2 cup chili sauce
1/3 cup ketchup
1/3 cup Worcestershire sauce
5 garlic cloves, minced
1-1/2 teaspoons chili powder

In a large resealable plastic bag, combine the flour, salt and pepper. Add ribs in batches and shake to coat. In a large skillet, brown ribs in butter. Transfer to a 5-qt. slow cooker.

In the same skillet, combine the remaining ingredients. Cook and stir until mixture comes to a boil; pour over ribs (slow cooker will be full). Cover and cook on low for 9-10 hours or until meat is tender. **Yield:** 12-15 servings.

Chili Mac

MEATY SPAGHETTI SAUCE

Cook Time: 8 Hours

*Arlene Sommers,
Redmond, Washington*
My family always enjoyed my homemade spaghetti sauce, but it's so time-consuming to make on the stovetop. My busy grown daughter adapted my recipe to take advantage of her slow cooker. The flavorful sauce still receives compliments.

1 pound ground beef
1 pound bulk Italian sausage
1 medium green pepper, chopped
1 medium onion, chopped
8 garlic cloves, minced
3 cans (14-1/2 ounces *each*) Italian diced tomatoes, drained
2 cans (15 ounces *each*) tomato sauce
2 cans (6 ounces *each*) tomato paste
1/3 cup sugar
2 tablespoons Italian seasoning
1 tablespoon dried basil
2 teaspoons dried marjoram
1 teaspoon salt
1/2 teaspoon pepper
Hot cooked spaghetti

In a large skillet over medium heat, cook beef and sausage until no longer pink; drain. Transfer to a 5-qt. slow cooker. Stir in green pepper, onion, garlic, tomatoes, tomato sauce, paste, sugar and seasonings; mix well. Cover and cook on low for 8 hours or until bubbly. Serve over spaghetti. **Yield:** 12 servings.

TACO MEAT LOAF

Cook Time: 8 Hours

*Diane Essinger
Findlay, Ohio*
Our children think there are three basic food groups—pizza, tacos and burgers! They like to doctor up slices of this specially seasoned meat loaf with their favorite taco toppings. It's a tasty meal we all enjoy.

1 egg
1/2 cup sour cream
1/3 cup salsa
2 to 4 tablespoons taco seasoning
1 cup crushed tortilla chips
1/2 cup shredded cheddar cheese
2 pounds lean ground beef
Optional toppings: sour cream, salsa, shredded cheddar cheese, shredded lettuce, sliced ripe olives

In a large bowl, combine the first six ingredients. Crumble beef over mixture and mix well. Pat into the bottom of a slow cooker.

Cover; cook on low for 8 hours or until a meat thermometer reads 160°. Top with sour cream, salsa, cheese, lettuce and olives if desired. **Yield:** 8 servings.

Meaty Spaghetti Sauce

Meatball Cabbage Rolls

MEATBALL CABBAGE ROLLS

Cook Time: 8 Hours

1 large head cabbage, cored
2 cans (one 8 ounces, one 15 ounces) tomato sauce, *divided*
1 small onion, chopped
1/3 cup uncooked long grain rice
2 tablespoons chili powder
Salt and garlic powder to taste
1 pound ground beef

In a Dutch oven, cook cabbage in boiling water only until the outer leaves fall off head, about 3 minutes. Remove cabbage from water and remove as many leaves as will come off easily. Reserve 14-16 large leaves for rolls. Return cabbage to water if more leaves are needed. Remove the thick vein from each leaf. In a bowl, combine 8 oz. of tomato sauce, onion, rice, chili powder, salt and garlic powder. Crumble beef over mixture; mix well. Shape into 2-in. balls. Place one meatball on each cabbage leaf; fold in sides. Starting at an unfolded edge, roll up leaf to completely enclose meatball. Secure with toothpicks.

Place in a 5-qt. slow cooker. Pour remaining tomato sauce over cabbage rolls. Cover and cook on low for 8 hours or until meat is no longer pink and cabbage is tender. Discard toothpicks. **Yield:** 4-6 servings.

Betty Buckmaster
Muskogee, Oklahoma
My mother would often have these cabbage rolls simmering in her slow cooker when my family and I arrived at her house for weekend visits. The mouth-watering meatballs tucked inside make these stand out from any other cabbage rolls I've tried.

GONE-ALL-DAY CASSEROLE

Cook Time: 6 to 8 Hours

1 cup uncooked wild rice, rinsed and drained
1 cup chopped celery
1 cup chopped carrots
2 cans (4 ounces *each*) mushroom stems and pieces, drained
1 large onion, chopped
1 garlic clove, minced
1/2 cup slivered almonds
3 beef bouillon cubes
2-1/2 teaspoons seasoned salt
2 pounds boneless round steak, cut into 1-inch cubes
3 cups water

Place ingredients in a slow cooker in the order listed (do not stir). Cover and cook on low for 6-8 hours or until rice is tender. Stir before serving. **Yield:** 12 servings.

Janet Haak Aarness
Pelican Rapids, Minnesota
Even less expensive cuts of meat become wonderfully tender when cooked slowly in this savory casserole. Wild rice and almonds add flair.

Spiced Pot Roast

SPICED POT ROAST

Cook Time: 8 to 9 Hours

1 boneless beef chuck roast
  (about 2-1/2 pounds)
1 medium onion, chopped
1 can (14-1/2 ounces) diced
  tomatoes, undrained
1/4 cup white vinegar
3 tablespoons tomato puree
2 teaspoons Dijon mustard
1/2 teaspoon lemon juice
4-1/2 teaspoons poppy seeds
2 garlic cloves, minced
2-1/4 teaspoons sugar
1/2 teaspoon ground ginger
1/2 teaspoon salt
1/2 teaspoon dried rosemary,
  crushed
1/4 teaspoon ground turmeric
1/4 teaspoon ground cumin
1/4 teaspoon crushed red pepper
  flakes
1/8 teaspoon ground cloves
1 bay leaf
Hot cooked noodles

Place roast in a slow cooker. In a large bowl, combine the onion, tomatoes, vinegar, tomato puree, mustard, lemon juice and seasonings; pour over roast.

Cover and cook on low for 8-9 hours or until meat is tender. Discard bay leaf. Thicken cooking juices if desired. Serve over noodles. **Yield:** 6-8 servings.

*Loren Martin
Big Cabin, Oklahoma
Just pour these ingredients over your pot roast and let the slow cooker do the work. Herbs and spices give the beef an excellent taste. I often serve this roast over noodles or with mashed potatoes, using the juices as a gravy.*

CUBE STEAKS WITH GRAVY

Cook Time: 8-1/2 Hours

Judy Long
Limestone, Tennessee
*With this recipe, good
flavor doesn't take
a back seat to conve-
nience. Cube steaks can
be tough and chewy.
But fixed this way,
they're a tender and
tasty family favorite.*

1/3 cup all-purpose flour
6 beef cube steaks (1-1/2 pounds)
1 tablespoon vegetable oil
1 large onion, sliced and separated into rings
3 cups water, *divided*
1 envelope brown gravy mix
1 envelope mushroom gravy mix
1 envelope onion gravy mix
Hot mashed potatoes *or* cooked noodles

Place flour in a large resealable plastic bag. Add steaks, a few at a time, and shake until completely coated. In a skillet, cook steaks in oil until lightly browned on each side. Transfer to a slow cooker. Add the onion and 2 cups water. Cover and cook on low for 8 hours or until meat is tender.

In a bowl, whisk together gravy mixes with remaining water. Add to slow cooker; cook 30 minutes longer. Serve over mashed potatoes or noodles. **Yield:** 6 servings.

STEAK 'N' GRAVY

Cook Time: 8-1/2 Hours

Betty Janway
Ruston, Louisiana
*Served over rice or
mashed potatoes, this
nicely spiced steak
makes a satisfying
meal. I like how tender
economical round steak
is when it comes out of
the slow cooker.*

1 pound round steak, trimmed
1 tablespoon vegetable oil
1-1/2 cups water
1 can (8 ounces) tomato sauce
1 teaspoon ground cumin
1 teaspoon garlic powder
1/2 teaspoon salt
1/4 teaspoon pepper
2 tablespoons all-purpose flour
1/4 cup cold water
Hot cooked rice *or* mashed potatoes

Cut the beef into bite-size pieces; brown in oil in a skillet. Transfer to a slow cooker. Cover with water; add the tomato sauce and seasonings. Cover and cook on low for 8 hours or until meat is tender.

In a small bowl, combine the flour and cold water to make a paste; stir into liquid in the slow cooker. Cover and cook on high 30 minutes longer or until the gravy is thickened. Serve over rice or potatoes. **Yield:** 4 servings.

Cube Steaks with Gravy

Easy-Does-It Spaghetti

Cook Time: 5 Hours

Genevieve Hrabe
Plainville, Kansas
This savory spaghetti sauce is a nice change from some of the sweeter store-bought varieties. With fresh bread and a green salad, you have a complete meal.

2 pounds ground beef, cooked and drained
1 can (46 ounces) tomato juice
1 can (15 ounces) tomato sauce
1 can (8 ounces) mushroom stems and pieces, drained
2 tablespoons dried minced onion
2 teaspoons salt
1 teaspoon garlic powder
1 teaspoon ground mustard
1/2 teaspoon *each* ground allspice, mace and pepper
1 package (7 ounces) spaghetti, broken in half

In a slow cooker, combine beef, tomato juice, tomato sauce, mushrooms and seasonings; mix well. Cover and cook on high for 4 hours. Stir in spaghetti. Cover and cook 1 hour longer or until the spaghetti is tender. **Yield:** 8-10 servings.

Garlic Beef Stroganoff

Cook Time: 7 to 8 Hours

Erika Anderson
Wausau, Wisconsin
I'm a mom and work full time, so I try to use my slow cooker whenever possible. This Stroganoff is perfect because I can get it ready in the morning before the kids get up.

2 teaspoons beef bouillon granules
1 cup boiling water
1 can (10-3/4 ounces) condensed cream of mushroom soup, undiluted
2 jars (4-1/2 ounces *each*) sliced mushrooms, drained
1 large onion, chopped
3 garlic cloves, minced
1 tablespoon Worcestershire sauce
1-1/2 to 2 pounds boneless round steak, trimmed and cut into thin strips
2 tablespoons vegetable oil
1 package (8 ounces) cream cheese, cubed
Hot cooked noodles

In a slow cooker, dissolve bouillon in water. Add next five ingredients. In a skillet, brown beef in oil. Transfer to slow cooker. Cover and cook on low for 7-8 hours or until the meat is tender. Stir in cream cheese until smooth. Serve over noodles. **Yield:** 6-8 servings.

Easy-Does-It Spaghetti

Round Steak Roll-Ups

ROUND STEAK ROLL-UPS

Cook Time: 6 Hours

2 pounds boneless beef round
   steak
1/2 cup grated carrot
1/3 cup chopped zucchini
1/4 cup chopped sweet
   red pepper
1/4 cup chopped green pepper
1/4 cup sliced green onions
2 tablespoons grated Parmesan
   cheese
1 tablespoon minced fresh
   parsley *or* 1 teaspoon dried
   parsley flakes
1 garlic clove, minced
1/4 teaspoon salt
1/4 teaspoon pepper
2 tablespoons canola oil
1 jar (14 ounces) meatless
   spaghetti sauce
Hot cooked spaghetti
Additional Parmesan cheese,
   optional

Cut meat into six pieces; pound to 1/4-in. thickness. Combine the vegetables, Parmesan cheese and seasonings; place 1/3 cup in the center of each piece. Roll meat up around filling; secure with toothpicks.

In a large skillet, brown roll-ups in oil over medium-high heat. Transfer to a 5-qt. slow cooker; top with spaghetti sauce. Cover and cook on low for 6 hours or until meat is tender. Discard toothpicks. Serve roll-ups and sauce over spaghetti. Sprinkle with the additional Parmesan if desired. **Yield:** 6 servings.

Kimberly Alonge
Westfield, New York
Since I'm a working mom, I like to assemble these tasty steak rolls the night before and pop them in the slow cooker the next morning before we're all out the door. They make a great meal after a long day.

Why Pay More?

Economical, less tender cuts of beef like round steak, stew meat and cube steak are perfect for the slow cooker. The long, slow cooking process achieved with the use of this handy appliance ensures fork-tender, moist and flavorful meat even on cuts that would be tough and chewy prepared using other cooking methods.

Apple & Onion Beef Pot Roast

Apple & Onion Beef Pot Roast

Cook Time: 5 to 6 Hours

1 boneless beef sirloin tip roast
   (3 pounds), cut in half
1 cup water
1 teaspoon seasoned salt
1/2 teaspoon reduced-sodium soy
   sauce
1/2 teaspoon Worcestershire
   sauce
1/4 teaspoon garlic powder
1 large tart apple, quartered
1 large onion, sliced
2 tablespoons cornstarch
2 tablespoons cold water
1/8 teaspoon browning sauce

In a large nonstick skillet coated with nonstick cooking spray, brown roast on all sides. Transfer to a 5-qt. slow cooker. Add water to the skillet, stirring to loosen any browned bits; pour over roast. Sprinkle with seasoned salt, soy sauce, Worcestershire sauce and garlic powder. Top with apple and onion. Cover and cook on low for 5-6 hours or until the meat is tender.

Remove roast and onion; let stand for 15 minutes before slicing. Strain cooking liquid into a saucepan, discarding apple. Bring liquid to a boil; cook until reduced to 2 cups, about 15 minutes. Combine cornstarch and cold water until smooth; stir in browning sauce. Stir into cooking liquid. Bring to a boil; cook and stir for 2 minutes or until thickened. Serve over beef and onion. **Yield:** 8 servings.

Rachel Koistinen
Hayti, South Dakota
Rely on your slow cooker to help prepare this moist pot roast. I thicken the juices to make a pleasing apple gravy that's wonderful over the beef slices and onions.

BEEFY AU GRATIN POTATOES

Cook Time: 4 Hours

Eileen Majerus
Pine Island, Minnesota
It's easy to vary the flavor of this hearty family-favorite casserole by using different kinds of soup and potato mixes. We enjoy the comforting combination of beef, potatoes and vegetables in this dish. I usually serve up heaping helpings with a salad and garlic bread.

1 package (5-1/4 ounces) au gratin *or* cheddar and bacon potatoes
1 can (15-1/4 ounces) whole kernel corn, drained
1 can (10-3/4 ounces) condensed cream of potato soup, undiluted
1 cup water
1 can (4 ounces) chopped green chilies, drained
1 can (4 ounces) mushroom stems and pieces, drained
1 jar (4 ounces) diced pimientos, drained
1 pound ground beef
1 medium onion, chopped

Set potato sauce mix aside. Place potatoes in a slow cooker; top with corn. In a bowl, combine the soup, water, chilies, mushrooms, pimientos and reserved sauce mix; mix well. Pour a third of the mixture over corn.

In a skillet, cook beef and onion over medium heat until the meat is no longer pink; drain. Transfer to slow cooker. Top with the remaining sauce mixture. Do not stir. Cover and cook on low for 4 hours or until potatoes are tender. **Yield:** 4-6 servings.

It's Best to Brown

For the best color and flavor, ground beef should be browned before using it in a slow cooker recipe. The exception is when preparing a meat loaf or similar dish.

Although it's not necessary to brown other cuts of meat or poultry, the process can enhance the flavor and appearance and reduce the fat in the finished dish.

CHICKEN & TURKEY

CHAPTER 5

ROSEMARY CASHEW CHICKEN

Cook Time: 4 to 5 Hours

Ruth Andrewson
Peck, Idaho
This elegant entree with
delicious herb flavor is
mouth-watering.
Cashews add richness
and crunch.

1 broiler/fryer chicken
(3 to 4 pounds), cut up and
skin removed
1 medium onion, thinly sliced
1/3 cup orange juice concentrate
1 teaspoon dried rosemary,
crushed
1 teaspoon salt
1/4 teaspoon cayenne pepper
2 tablespoons all-purpose flour
3 tablespoons water
1/4 to 1/2 cup chopped cashews
Hot cooked pasta

Place chicken in a slow cooker. Combine onion, orange juice concentrate, rosemary, salt and cayenne; pour over chicken. Cover and cook on low for 4-5 hours or until chicken juices run clear. Remove the chicken and keep warm.

In a saucepan, combine flour and water until smooth. Stir in cooking juices. Bring to a boil; cook and stir for 2 minutes or until thickened. Stir in cashews. Pour over chicken. Serve with pasta. **Yield:** 4-6 servings.

SLOW COOKER CHICKEN DINNER

Cook Time: 8-1/2 Hours

Jenet Cattar
Neptune Beach, Florida
This meal-in-one, which
includes juicy chicken
and tasty veggies in a
creamy sauce, is ready to
eat when I get home
from the office. It's great
to walk in the door and
smell this cooking.

6 medium red potatoes, cut into
chunks
4 medium carrots, cut
into 1/2-inch pieces
4 boneless skinless chicken
breast halves
1 can (10-3/4 ounces) condensed
cream of chicken soup,
undiluted
1 can (10-3/4 ounces) condensed
cream of mushroom soup,
undiluted

1/8 teaspoon garlic salt
2 to 4 tablespoons mashed
potato flakes, optional

Place potatoes and carrots in a slow cooker. Top with chicken. Combine the soups and garlic salt; pour over chicken. Cover and cook on low for 8 hours. To thicken if desired, stir potato flakes into the gravy and cook 30 minutes longer. **Yield:** 4 servings.

Rosemary Cashew Chicken

No-Fuss Chicken

Cook Time: 2 to 2-1/2 Hours

Sandra Flick
Toledo, Ohio
My mother-in-law devised this recipe when her children were growing up. It was a favorite Sunday dish because it could cook while the family was at church. When they came home, it didn't take long to put dinner on the table.

2/3 cup all-purpose flour
1 teaspoon dried sage
1 teaspoon dried basil
1 teaspoon seasoned salt
1 broiler/fryer chicken (2-1/2 to 3 pounds), cut up
1/4 cup butter
2 cups chicken broth

In a shallow bowl, combine flour, sage, basil and seasoned salt; coat chicken. Reserve remaining flour mixture. In a large skillet, melt butter; brown chicken on all sides. Transfer to a slow cooker.

Add 1/4 cup reserved flour mixture to the skillet (discarding the rest); stir until smooth. When mixture begins to bubble, stir in chicken broth and bring to a boil; boil for 1 minute. Pour over chicken. Cover and cook on high for 2 to 2-1/2 hours or until chicken juices run clear. **Yield:** 4 servings.

Creamy Italian Chicken

Cook Time: 4 Hours

Maura McGee
Tallahassee, Florida
This tender chicken in a creamy sauce gets fast flavor from a salad dressing mix. Served over rice or pasta, it's rich, delicious and special enough for company.

4 boneless skinless chicken breast halves
1 envelope Italian salad dressing mix
1/4 cup water
1 package (8 ounces) cream cheese, softened
1 can (10-3/4 ounces) condensed cream of chicken soup, undiluted
1 can (4 ounces) mushroom stems and pieces, drained
Hot cooked rice or noodles

Place the chicken in a slow cooker. Combine salad dressing mix and water; pour over chicken. Cover and cook on low for 3 hours. In a small mixing bowl, beat cream cheese and soup until blended. Stir in mushrooms. Pour over chicken. Cook 1 hour longer or until chicken juices run clear. Serve over rice or noodles. **Yield:** 4 servings.

No-Fuss Chicken

SAUCY APRICOT CHICKEN

Cook Time: 4 to 5 Hours

6 boneless skinless chicken
   breast halves (about 1-1/2
   pounds)
2 jars (12 ounces *each*) apricot
   preserves
1 envelope onion soup mix
Hot cooked rice

Place chicken in a slow cooker. Combine the preserves and soup mix; spoon over chicken. Cover and cook on low for 4-5 hours or until tender. Serve over rice. **Yield:** 6 servings.

Dee Gray
Kokomo, Indiana
Just four ingredients are all you'll need for a scrumptious chicken entree. The tangy glaze is just as wonderful with ham or turkey.

SUNDAY CHICKEN SUPPER

Cook Time: 6 to 8 Hours

4 medium carrots, cut
   into 2-inch pieces
1 medium onion, chopped
1 celery rib, cut into 2-inch
   pieces
2 cups cut fresh green beans
   (2-inch pieces)
5 small red potatoes, quartered
2 to 4 tablespoons vegetable oil
1 broiler/fryer chicken
   (3 to 3-1/2 pounds), cut up
4 bacon strips, cooked and
   crumbled
1-1/2 cups hot water
2 teaspoons chicken bouillon
   granules
1 teaspoon salt

1/2 teaspoon dried thyme
1/2 teaspoon dried basil
Pinch pepper

In a 5-qt. slow cooker, layer first five ingredients in order listed. In a skillet, heat oil; brown the chicken on all sides. Transfer to a slow cooker; top with bacon.

In a bowl, combine remaining ingredients; pour over top. Do not stir. Cover; cook on low for 6-8 hours or until vegetables are tender and chicken juices run clear. Remove chicken and vegetables.

If desired, thicken juices for gravy in a saucepan. Return chicken and vegetables to slow cooker. Drizzle with gravy. **Yield:** 4 servings.

Ruthann Martin
Louisville, Ohio
This yummy slow-cooked sensation is loaded with chicken, vegetables and seasonings. It's a dish that satisfies the biggest appetites.

Creamy Chicken Fettuccine

CREAMY CHICKEN FETTUCCINE

Cook Time: 3 to 4 Hours

1-1/2 pounds boneless skinless
    chicken breasts, cut into cubes
1/2 teaspoon garlic powder
1/2 teaspoon onion powder
1/8 teaspoon pepper
  1 can (10-3/4 ounces) condensed
    cream of chicken soup,
    undiluted
  1 can (10-3/4 ounces) condensed
    cream of celery soup,
    undiluted
  4 ounces process cheese
    (Velveeta), cubed
  1 can (2-1/4 ounces) sliced ripe
    olives, drained
  1 jar (2 ounces) diced pimientos,
    drained, optional
  1 package (16 ounces) spinach
    fettuccine *or* spaghetti
Thin breadsticks, optional

Place the chicken in a slow cooker; sprinkle with garlic powder, onion powder and pepper. Top with soups. Cover and cook on high for 3-4 hours or until chicken juices run clear. Stir in the cheese, olives and pimientos if desired. Cover and cook until the cheese is melted.

Meanwhile, cook fettuccine according to package directions; drain. Serve with the chicken and breadsticks if desired. **Yield:** 6 servings.

Melissa Cowser
Greenville, Texas
Convenient canned soup and process cheese hurry along the assembly of this creamy sauce loaded with delicious chunks of chicken.

You've Got Good Taste

Always taste the finished dish before serving to adjust seasonings to your preference, since long cooking times can dilute the strength of herbs and spices. Consider adding a dash of salt, pepper, lemon juice or minced fresh herbs.

SLOW-COOKED ORANGE CHICKEN

Cook Time: 4-1/2 Hours

Nancy Wit
Fremont, Nebraska
Everyone who tries this saucy chicken likes the taste, including my grandchildren. A hint of orange gives the chicken a delicious flavor. It travels well, and I often take it to potluck suppers.

1 broiler/fryer chicken (3 pounds), cut up and skin removed
3 cups orange juice
1 cup chopped celery
1 cup chopped green pepper
1 can (4 ounces) mushroom stems and pieces, drained
4 teaspoons dried minced onion
1 teaspoon dried parsley flakes
1/2 teaspoon salt
1/4 teaspoon pepper
3 tablespoons cornstarch
3 tablespoons cold water
Hot cooked rice, optional

Combine the first nine ingredients in a slow cooker. Cover and cook on low for 4 hours or until meat juices run clear. Combine cornstarch and water until smooth; stir into cooking juices. Cover and cook on high for 30-45 minutes or until thickened. Serve over rice if desired. **Yield:** 4 servings.

TURKEY IN CREAM SAUCE

Cook Time: 7 to 8 Hours

Kathy-Jo Winterbottom
Pottstown, Pennsylvania
I've been relying on this recipe for tender turkey since I first moved out on my own years ago. I serve it whenever I invite new guests to the house, and I'm constantly sharing the recipe.

1-1/4 cups white wine *or* chicken broth
1 medium onion, chopped
2 garlic cloves, minced
2 bay leaves
2 teaspoons dried rosemary, crushed
1/2 teaspoon pepper
3 turkey breast tenderloins (3/4 pound *each*)
3 tablespoons cornstarch
1/2 cup half-and-half cream *or* milk
1/2 teaspoon salt

In a slow cooker, combine wine or broth, onion, garlic and bay leaves. Combine rosemary and pepper; rub over turkey. Place in slow cooker. Cover; cook on low 7-8 hours or until meat is tender. Remove turkey; keep warm. Strain cooking juices; pour into a saucepan.

Combine cornstarch, cream and salt until smooth; gradually add to juices. Bring to a boil; cook and stir 2 minutes or until thickened. Slice turkey; serve with sauce. **Yield:** 9 servings.

Slow-Cooked Orange Chicken

Stuffed Chicken Rolls

STUFFED CHICKEN ROLLS

Cook Time: 4 to 5 Hours

6 boneless skinless chicken
    breast halves
6 slices fully cooked ham
6 slices Swiss cheese
1/4 cup all-purpose flour
1/4 cup grated Parmesan cheese
1/2 teaspoon rubbed sage
1/4 teaspoon paprika
1/4 teaspoon pepper
1/4 cup vegetable oil
1 can (10-3/4 ounces) condensed
    cream of chicken soup,
    undiluted
1/2 cup chicken broth
Chopped fresh parsley, optional

Flatten chicken to 1/8-in. thickness. Place 1 slice ham and cheese on each breast. Roll up and tuck in ends; secure with a toothpick. Combine the flour, Parmesan cheese, sage, paprika and pepper; coat chicken on all sides. Cover and refrigerate for 1 hour.

In a large skillet, brown chicken in oil over medium-high heat. Transfer to a 5-qt. slow cooker. Combine soup and broth; pour over chicken. Cover and cook on low for 4-5 hours. Remove toothpicks. Garnish with parsley if desired. **Yield:** 6 servings.

Jean Sherwood
Kenneth City, Florida
The wonderful aroma of this moist delicious chicken cooking sparks our appetites. The ham and cheese rolled inside is a tasty surprise. When I prepared this impressive main dish for a church luncheon, I received lots of compliments. The rolls are especially nice served over rice or pasta.

SOUTHWESTERN CHICKEN

Cook Time: 3 to 4 Hours

2 cans (15-1/4 ounces *each*)
    whole kernel corn, drained
1 can (15 ounces) black beans,
    rinsed and drained
1 jar (16 ounces) chunky salsa,
    divided
6 boneless skinless chicken
    breast halves
1 cup (4 ounces) shredded
    cheddar cheese

Combine the corn, black beans and 1/2 cup of salsa in a slow cooker. Top with chicken; pour the remaining salsa over chicken. Cover and cook on high for 3-4 hours or on low for 7-8 hours or until meat juices run clear. Sprinkle with cheese; cover until cheese is melted, about 5 minutes. **Yield:** 6 servings.

Karen Waters
Laurel, Maryland
Prepared salsa and convenient canned corn and beans add fun color, texture and flavor to this tender chicken dish. I serve it with rice and a salad. Our children love it.

Chicken with Vegetables

Chicken with Vegetables

Cook Time: 5 Hours

1 cup sliced fresh mushrooms
4 chicken legs, skin removed
4 chicken thighs, skin removed
4 celery ribs, sliced
1 cup sliced zucchini
1 cup sliced carrots
1 medium onion, sliced
1 cup tomato juice
1/2 cup chicken broth
1 garlic clove, minced
1/4 teaspoon paprika
Pepper to taste
3 tablespoons cornstarch
3 tablespoons cold water
Hot cooked rice

Place mushrooms and chicken in a slow cooker. Add the celery, zucchini, carrots, onion, tomato juice, broth, garlic, paprika and pepper. Cover and cook on low for 5 hours or until meat juices run clear.

Remove chicken and vegetables and keep warm. Transfer cooking juices to a saucepan; skim fat. Combine the cornstarch and water until smooth; add to the juices. Bring to a boil; cook and stir for 2 minutes or until thickened. Pour over chicken and vegetables; serve over rice. **Yield:** 4 servings.

Norlene Razak
Tye, Texas
You'll be surprised at how easily this tender chicken entree comes together. It's simple, delicious and a great way to get your family to eat vegetables.

King-Size Drumsticks

Cook Time: 8 to 10 Hours

1 can (10 ounces) enchilada sauce
1 can (4 ounces) chopped green
  chilies, drained
1 teaspoon dried oregano
1/2 teaspoon garlic salt
1/2 teaspoon ground cumin
6 turkey drumsticks
3 tablespoons cornstarch
3 tablespoons cold water

In a bowl, combine first five ingredients. Place the drumsticks in a 5-qt. slow cooker; top with sauce. Cover; cook on low for 8-10 hours or until a meat thermometer reads 180°.

Remove turkey and keep warm. Strain sauce into a saucepan. Combine cornstarch and water until smooth; stir into the pan. Bring to a boil; cook and stir for 2 minutes or until thickened. Serve with turkey. **Yield:** 6 servings.

Taste of Home's
Test Kitchen
Let your slow cooker do the work for you when you serve these savory turkey legs. In this recipe, enchilada sauce, green chilies and cumin give this main dish a zesty royal treatment.

Turkey in a Pot

TURKEY IN A POT

Cook Time: 5 to 6 Hours

1 boneless turkey breast
   (3 to 4 pounds), halved
1 can (16 ounces) whole-berry
   cranberry sauce
1/2 cup sugar
1/2 cup apple juice
1 tablespoon cider vinegar
2 garlic cloves, minced
1 teaspoon ground mustard
1/2 teaspoon ground cinnamon
1/4 teaspoon ground cloves
1/4 teaspoon ground allspice
2 tablespoons all-purpose flour
1/4 cup cold water
1/4 teaspoon browning sauce,
   optional

Place the turkey skin side up in a 5-qt. slow cooker. Combine cranberry sauce, sugar, apple juice, vinegar, garlic, mustard, cinnamon, cloves and allspice; pour over turkey. Cover and cook on low for 5-6 hours or until a meat thermometer reads 170°.

Remove turkey to a cutting board; keep warm. Strain cooking juices. In a saucepan, combine flour and water until smooth; gradually stir in strained juices. Bring to a boil; cook and stir for 2 minutes or until thickened. Stir in browning sauce if desired. Serve with sliced turkey. **Yield:** 12-16 servings.

Lois Woodward
Okeechobee, Florida
I use this recipe often for an easy Sunday dinner. The turkey breast gets a "holiday treatment" when served with cranberry gravy seasoned with cinnamon, cloves and allspice.

CHICKEN WITH STUFFING

Cook Time: 4 Hours

4 boneless skinless chicken
   breast halves
1 can (10-3/4 ounces) condensed
   cream of chicken soup,
   undiluted
1-1/4 cups water
1/4 cup butter, melted
1 package (6 ounces) corn bread
   stuffing mix

Place chicken in a greased slow cooker. Top with soup. In a bowl, combine the water, butter and stuffing mix; spoon over the chicken. Cover and cook on low for 4 hours or until chicken juices run clear. **Yield:** 4 servings.

Susan Kutz
Valley, Illinois
I need only five ingredients to create this comforting chicken topped with corn bread stuffing.

Sage Turkey Thighs

Cook Time: 6 to 8 Hours

Natalie Swanson
Catonsville, Maryland
I created this for my boys, who love dark meat. It's more convenient than cooking a whole turkey. It reminds me of our traditional Thanksgiving turkey and stuffing seasoned with sage.

4 medium carrots, halved
1 medium onion, chopped
1/2 cup water
2 garlic cloves, minced
1-1/2 teaspoons rubbed sage, divided
2 turkey thighs or drumsticks (about 2 pounds), skin removed
1 teaspoon browning sauce, optional
1/4 teaspoon salt
1/8 teaspoon pepper
1 tablespoon cornstarch
1/4 cup cold water

In a slow cooker, combine the carrots, onion, water, garlic and 1 teaspoon sage. Top with turkey. Sprinkle with the remaining sage. Cover and cook on low for 6-8 hours or until a meat thermometer reads 180°.

Remove turkey and keep warm. Skim fat from cooking juices; strain and reserve vegetables. Place vegetables in a food processor; cover and process until smooth. Place in a saucepan; add cooking juices. Bring to a boil. Add browning sauce if desired, salt and pepper.

Combine the cornstarch and water until smooth; add to the juices. Bring to a boil; cook and stir for 2 minutes or until thickened. Serve with the turkey. **Yield:** 4 servings.

Sage Turkey Thighs

Turkey Enchiladas

Cook Time: 6 to 8 Hours

Stella Schams
Tempe, Arizona
I was pleased to discover a different way to serve an economical cut of meat. I simmer turkey thighs with tomato sauce, green chilies and seasonings until they're tender and flavorful. Then I shred the turkey and serve it in tortillas with other fresh fixings.

2 turkey thighs *or* drumsticks (about 2 pounds)
1 can (8 ounces) tomato sauce
1 can (4 ounces) chopped green chilies
1/3 cup chopped onion
2 tablespoons Worcestershire sauce
1 to 2 tablespoons chili powder
1/4 teaspoon garlic powder
8 flour tortillas (7 inches)
Chopped green onions, sliced ripe olives, chopped tomatoes, shredded cheddar cheese, sour cream *and/or* shredded lettuce

Remove skin from the turkey. Place in a 5-qt. slow cooker. Combine the tomato sauce, chilies, onion, Worcestershire sauce, chili powder and garlic powder; pour over turkey. Cover; cook on low for 6-8 hours or until the turkey is tender.

Remove the turkey; shred the meat with a fork and return to the slow cooker. Heat through. Spoon about 1/2 cup of the turkey mixture down the center of each tortilla. Add the toppings of your choice. Fold bottom of the tortilla over the filling and roll up. **Yield:** 4 servings.

Red Pepper Chicken

Cook Time: 6 Hours

Piper Spiwak
Vienna, Virginia
Chicken breasts are treated to a bevy of black beans, red peppers and tomatoes in this Southwestern supper. We love this colorful dish over rice cooked in chicken broth.

4 boneless skinless chicken breast halves
1 can (15 ounces) black beans, rinsed and drained
1 jar (15 ounces) roasted red peppers, undrained
1 can (14-1/2 ounces) Mexican stewed tomatoes, undrained
1 large onion, chopped
1/2 teaspoon salt
Pepper to taste
Hot cooked rice

Place the chicken in a slow cooker. In a bowl, combine the beans, red peppers, tomatoes, onion, salt and pepper. Pour over the chicken.

Cover and cook on low for 6 hours or until chicken juices run clear. Serve over rice. **Yield:** 4 servings.

Turkey Enchiladas

Turkey with Mushroom Sauce

Cook Time: 7 to 8 Hours

Myra Innes
Auburn, Kansas
When we were first married, I didn't have an oven, so I made this tender turkey in the slow cooker. Now I rely on this recipe because it frees up the oven to make other dishes.

1 boneless turkey breast (3 pounds), halved
2 tablespoons butter, melted
2 tablespoons dried parsley flakes
1/2 teaspoon dried tarragon
1/2 teaspoon salt
1/8 teaspoon pepper
1 jar (4-1/2 ounces) sliced mushrooms, drained *or* 1 cup sliced fresh mushrooms
1/2 cup white wine *or* chicken broth
2 tablespoons cornstarch
1/4 cup cold water

Place the turkey, skin side up, in a slow cooker. Brush with butter. Sprinkle with parsley, tarragon, salt and pepper. Top with mushrooms. Pour wine or broth over all. Cover and cook on low for 7-8 hours. Remove turkey and keep warm. Skim fat from cooking juices.

In a saucepan, combine the cornstarch and water until smooth. Gradually add the cooking juices. Bring to a boil; cook and stir for 2 minutes or until thickened. Serve with the turkey. **Yield:** 12 servings (2-1/2 cups sauce).

Turkey with Mushroom Sauce

Mandarin Chicken

Cook Time: 7-1/2 to 8-1/2 Hours

Aney Chatterton
Soda Springs, Idaho
Oranges and olives are
elegantly paired in this
different but delicious
dish. The chicken is
marinated, then cooked
slowly in a flavorful
sauce, so it stays moist.

1 broiler/fryer chicken
(3 to 3-1/2 pounds), cut up
and skin removed
2 cups water
1 cup ketchup
1/4 cup packed brown sugar
1/4 cup soy sauce
1/4 cup orange juice concentrate
2 teaspoons ground mustard
2 teaspoons salt
1 teaspoon pepper
1 teaspoon ground ginger
1 teaspoon garlic salt
3 tablespoons cornstarch
1/2 cup cold water
1 can (11 ounces) mandarin
oranges, drained
1/2 cup whole pitted ripe olives
2 tablespoons chopped green
pepper
Hot cooked rice

Place chicken in a large resealable plastic bag or glass dish. In a bowl, combine water, ketchup, brown sugar, soy sauce, orange juice concentrate, mustard, salt, pepper, ginger and garlic salt. Pour half over the chicken. Cover chicken and remaining marinade; refrigerate for 8 hours or overnight. Drain chicken, discarding marinade.

Place chicken in a slow cooker; add reserved marinade. Cover and cook on low for 7-8 hours. Combine cornstarch and cold water until smooth; stir into the chicken mixture. Add oranges, olives and green pepper. Cover and cook on high for 30-45 minutes or until thickened. Serve over rice. **Yield:** 4-6 servings.

PORK, LAMB & SEAFOOD

Sunday Pot Roast

Cook Time: 8 Hours

Brandy Schaefer
Glen Carbon, Illinois
This recipe proves you don't have to stand over a hot stove to prepare a delicious down-home dinner like Grandma used to make. The roast turns out moist and tasty every time.

1 teaspoon dried oregano
1/2 teaspoon onion salt
1/2 teaspoon pepper
1/2 teaspoon caraway seed
1/4 teaspoon garlic salt
1 boneless pork loin roast (3-1/2 to 4 pounds), trimmed
6 medium carrots, peeled and cut into 1-1/2-inch pieces
3 large potatoes, peeled and quartered
3 small onions, quartered
1-1/2 cups beef broth
1/3 cup all-purpose flour
1/3 cup cold water
1/4 teaspoon browning sauce, optional

Combine the seasonings; rub over roast. Wrap in plastic wrap and refrigerate overnight. Place carrots, potatoes and onions in a slow cooker; add broth. Unwrap roast and place in the slow cooker. Cover and cook on high for 2 hours. Reduce heat to low and cook 6 hours longer or until a meat thermometer reads 160°.

Transfer the roast and vegetables to a serving platter; keep warm. Pour broth into a saucepan. Combine the flour and water until smooth; stir into broth. Bring to a boil; boil and whisk for 2 minutes. Add the browning sauce if desired. Serve with the roast. **Yield:** 12-14 servings.

Time to Toast

Toasting sesame seeds brings out a wonderful rich flavor that can complement many recipes and give a bit of crunch to saucy dishes prepared in the slow cooker. (See Sesame Pork Ribs on page 194.)

Toast sesame seeds in a dry skillet over medium heat for 10-15 minutes until they're lightly browned, stirring occasionally.

Or, bake them on an ungreased baking sheet at 350° for 10-15 minutes or until they're lightly browned. Watch carefully to avoid scorching.

Sunday Pot Roast

SESAME PORK RIBS

Cook Time: 5 to 6 Hours

Sandy Alexander
Fayetteville,
North Carolina
No one ever believes how little effort it takes to make these tasty tempting ribs. The flavor of the lightly sweet and tangy sauce penetrates through the meat as the ribs simmer in the slow cooker.

3/4 cup packed brown sugar
1/2 cup soy sauce
1/2 cup ketchup
1/4 cup honey
  2 tablespoons white wine vinegar
  3 garlic cloves, minced
  1 teaspoon ground ginger
  1 teaspoon salt
1/4 to 1/2 teaspoon crushed red pepper flakes
  5 pounds country-style pork ribs
  1 medium onion, sliced
  2 tablespoons sesame seeds, toasted
  2 tablespoons chopped green onions

In a large bowl, combine the first nine ingredients. Add ribs and turn to coat. Place onion in a 5-qt. slow cooker; arrange ribs on top and pour sauce over.

Cover and cook on low for 5-6 hours or until a meat thermometer reads 160°-170°. Place ribs on a serving platter; sprinkle with sesame seeds and green onions. **Yield:** 6 servings.

CHICKEN FRIED CHOPS

Cook Time: 6 to 8 Hours

Connie Slocum
Brunswick, Georgia
It takes only a few minutes to brown the meat before assembling this savory meal. The pork chops simmer all day in a flavorful sauce until they're fork-tender.

1/2 cup all-purpose flour
  2 teaspoons salt
1-1/2 teaspoons ground mustard
1/2 teaspoon garlic powder
  6 pork loin chops (3/4 inch thick), trimmed
  2 tablespoons vegetable oil
  1 can (10-3/4 ounces) condensed cream of chicken soup, undiluted
1/3 cup water

In a shallow bowl, combine flour, salt, mustard and garlic powder; dredge pork chops. In a skillet, brown the chops on both sides in oil. Place in a slow cooker. Combine soup and water; pour over the chops.

Cover and cook on low for 6-8 hours or until meat is tender. If desired, thicken pan juices and serve with the pork chops. **Yield:** 6 servings.

Sesame Pork Ribs

EASY AND ELEGANT HAM

Cook Time: 6 to 7 Hours

Denise DiPace
Medford, New Jersey
I fix this moist tender ham to serve my large family. Covered with colorful pineapple slices, cherries and orange glaze, its showstopping appearance and flavor appeal to both children and adults.

2 cans (20 ounces *each*) sliced pineapple
1 fully cooked boneless ham (about 6 pounds), halved
1 jar (6 ounces) maraschino cherries, well drained
1 jar (12 ounces) orange marmalade

Drain pineapple, reserving juice; set juice aside. Place half of the pineapple in an ungreased 5-qt. slow cooker. Top with the ham. Add cherries, remaining pineapple and reserved pineapple juice. Spoon marmalade over ham. Cover and cook on low for 6-7 hours or until heated through.

Remove to a warm serving platter. Let stand for 10-15 minutes before slicing. Serve the pineapple and cherries with the sliced ham. **Yield:** 18-20 servings.

PORK AND CABBAGE DINNER

Cook Time: 8 Hours

Trina Hinkel
Minneapolis, Minnesota
I put on this pork roast in the morning to avoid that evening dinner rush. All I do is fix potatoes, and our family can sit down to a satisfying supper.

1 pound carrots
1-1/2 cups water
1 envelope onion soup mix
2 garlic cloves, minced
1/2 teaspoon celery seed
1 boneless pork shoulder roast (4 to 6 pounds)
1/2 teaspoon salt
1/4 teaspoon pepper
1-1/2 pounds cabbage, cut into 2-inch pieces

Cut carrots in half lengthwise; then into 2-in. pieces. Place in a 5-qt. slow cooker. Add water, soup mix, garlic and celery seed. Cut roast in half; place over carrot mixture. Sprinkle with salt and pepper. Cover; cook on high for 2 hours.

Reduce heat to low; cook for 4 hours. Add cabbage; cook 2 hours longer or until the cabbage is tender and a meat thermometer reads 160°. Remove meat and vegetables to a serving plate; keep warm. If desired, thicken pan drippings for gravy and serve with the roast. **Yield:** 8-10 servings.

Easy and Elegant Ham

Teriyaki Pork Roast

Cook Time: 7 to 8 Hours

3/4 cup unsweetened apple juice
2 tablespoons sugar
2 tablespoons soy sauce
1 tablespoon vinegar
1 teaspoon ground ginger
1/4 teaspoon garlic powder
1/8 teaspoon pepper
1 boneless pork loin roast
(about 3 pounds), halved
7-1/2 teaspoons cornstarch
3 tablespoons cold water

Combine the first seven ingredients in a greased slow cooker. Add roast and turn to coat. Cover and cook on low for 7-8 hours or until a thermometer inserted into the roast reads 160°. Remove roast and keep warm.

In a saucepan, combine cornstarch and cold water until smooth; stir in cooking juices. Bring to a boil; cook and stir for 2 minutes or until thickened. Serve with the roast. **Yield:** 8 servings.

Roxanne Hulsey
Gainesville, Georgia
Since my husband works full time and attends school, I do a great deal around the house. I'm always looking for no-fuss recipes, so I was thrilled to find this one.

San Francisco Chops

Cook Time: 7-1/2 to 8-1/2 Hours

4 bone-in pork loin chops
(1 inch thick)
1 to 2 tablespoons vegetable oil
1 garlic clove, minced
1/4 cup soy sauce
1/4 cup red wine *or* chicken broth
2 tablespoons brown sugar
1/4 teaspoon crushed red pepper
flakes
1 tablespoon cornstarch
1 tablespoon cold water
Hot cooked rice

In a skillet, brown pork chops in oil; transfer to a slow cooker. Add garlic to drippings; cook and stir for about 1 minute or until golden. Stir in next four ingredients; cook and stir until sugar is dissolved. Pour over chops. Cover and cook on low for 7-8 hours or until meat is tender.

Remove chops. Combine cornstarch and cold water until smooth; gradually stir into slow cooker. Return chops to slow cooker. Cover and cook for at least 30 minutes or until slightly thickened. Serve over rice. **Yield:** 4 servings.

Tara Bonesteel
Dayton, New Jersey
It's easy to please friends and family with these fast-to-fix chops. Simmered in a tangy sauce all day, they're so moist and delicious by dinnertime they practically melt in your mouth.

Slow-Cooked Lamb Chops

Slow-Cooked Lamb Chops

Cook Time: 4 to 6 Hours

1 medium onion, sliced
1 teaspoon dried oregano
1/2 teaspoon dried thyme
1/2 teaspoon garlic powder
1/4 teaspoon salt
1/8 teaspoon pepper
8 loin lamb chops (about 1-3/4 pounds)
2 garlic cloves, minced

Place onion in a slow cooker. Combine oregano, thyme, garlic powder, salt and pepper; rub over the lamb chops. Place chops over onion. Top with garlic. Cover and cook on low for 4-6 hours or until the meat is tender. **Yield:** 4 servings.

Sandra McKenzie
Braham, Minnesota
Chops are without a doubt the cut of lamb we like best. The aroma is irresistible, and they come out of the slow cooker so tender.

Sesame Pork Roast

Cook Time: 9 to 10 Hours

1 boneless pork shoulder roast (4 pounds), trimmed
2 cups water
1/2 cup soy sauce
1/4 cup sesame seeds, toasted
1/4 cup molasses
1/4 cup white wine vinegar
4 green onions, sliced
2 teaspoons garlic powder
1/4 teaspoon cayenne pepper
3 tablespoons cornstarch
1/4 cup cold water

Cut roast in half; place in a large resealable plastic bag or glass dish. In a bowl, combine the water, soy sauce, sesame seeds, molasses, vinegar, onions, garlic powder and cayenne. Pour half over the roast. Cover pork and remaining marinade; refrigerate overnight.

Drain pork, discarding marinade. Place roast in a 5-qt. slow cooker; add reserved marinade. Cover; cook on high for 1 hour. Reduce temperature to low; cook 8-9 hours longer or until meat is tender. Remove roast and keep warm. In a saucepan, combine cornstarch and cold water until smooth; stir in cooking juices. Bring to a boil; cook and stir for 2 minutes. Serve with roast. **Yield:** 8 servings.

Sue Brown
San Miguel, California
I marinate a boneless cut of pork in a tangy sauce overnight before cooking it slowly the next day. The result is a tasty roast that's fall-apart tender.

Sweet and Savory Ribs

Sweet and Savory Ribs

Cook Time: 8 to 9 Hours

1 large onion, sliced and
   separated into rings
2-1/2 to 3 pounds boneless country-
   style pork ribs
1 bottle (18 ounces) honey
   barbecue sauce
1/3 cup maple syrup
1/4 cup spicy brown mustard
1/2 teaspoon salt
1/4 teaspoon pepper

Place onion in a 5-qt. slow cooker. Top with the ribs. Combine the barbecue sauce, syrup, mustard, salt and pepper; pour over ribs.

Cover and cook on low for 8-9 hours or until the meat is tender. **Yield:** 6-8 servings.

Kandy Bingham
Green River, Wyoming
My husband and I love barbecued ribs, but we rarely have time to fire up the grill. So we let the slow cooker do the work for us. By the time we get home from work, the ribs are tender and ready to devour.

Pork Chops and Beans

Cook Time: 8 to 9-1/2 Hours

4 pork loin chops (1/2 inch thick)
1/2 teaspoon salt
1/4 teaspoon pepper
1 tablespoon vegetable oil
2 medium onions, chopped
2 garlic cloves, minced
1/4 cup chili sauce
1-1/2 teaspoons brown sugar
1 teaspoon prepared mustard
1 can (16 ounces) kidney beans,
   rinsed and drained
1 can (15-1/4 ounces) lima
   beans, rinsed and drained

Sprinkle pork chops with salt and pepper. In a skillet, brown chops in oil; transfer chops to a slow cooker. Reserve 1 tablespoon drippings in the skillet; saute onions and garlic until tender. Stir in chili sauce, brown sugar and mustard. Pour over chops.

Cover and cook on low for 7-8 hours. Stir in beans. Cover and cook 1 to 1-1/2 hours longer or until meat juices run clear and beans are heated through. **Yield:** 4 servings.

Dorothy Pritchett
Wills Point, Texas
This hearty combination of juicy pork chops and two kinds of beans makes a satisfying supper from the slow cooker any time of year.

Slow Cooker Salmon Loaf

Slow Cooker Salmon Loaf

Cook Time: 4 to 6 Hours

2 eggs, lightly beaten
2 cups seasoned stuffing
  croutons
1 cup chicken broth
1 cup grated Parmesan cheese
1/4 teaspoon ground mustard
1 can (14-3/4 ounces) salmon,
  drained, bones and skin
  removed

In a bowl, combine the first five ingredients. Add salmon and mix well. Transfer to a slow cooker coated with nonstick cooking spray. Gently shape the mixture into a loaf.

Cover and cook on low for 4-6 hours or until a meat thermometer reads 160°. **Yield:** 6 servings.

Kelly Ritter
Douglasville, Georgia
I adapted this recipe from one I found in an old slow-cooker book of my grandma's. I serve it with macaroni and cheese and pinto beans.

Pizza in a Pot

Cook Time: 8 to 9 Hours

1 pound bulk Italian sausage
1 can (28 ounces) crushed
  tomatoes
1 can (15-1/2 ounces) chili beans
1 can (15 ounces) black beans,
  rinsed and drained
1 can (2-1/4 ounces) sliced ripe
  olives, drained
1 medium onion, chopped
1 small green pepper, chopped
2 garlic cloves, minced
1/4 cup grated Parmesan cheese
1 tablespoon quick-cooking
  tapioca
1 tablespoon dried basil

1 bay leaf
1 teaspoon salt
1/2 teaspoon sugar
Hot cooked pasta
Shredded mozzarella cheese, optional

In a skillet over medium heat, cook the sausage until no longer pink; drain. Transfer to a slow cooker. Add the next 13 ingredients; mix well.

Cover and cook on low for 8-9 hours or until slightly thickened. Discard bay leaf. Stir before serving over pasta. Sprinkle with mozzarella cheese if desired. **Yield:** 6-8 servings.

Anita Doughty
West Des Moines, Iowa
Since most kids will try anything to do with pizza, I rely on this recipe when one of my two teenage sons has a friend stay for dinner. It's frequently a hit.

SLOW-COOKED HAM

Cook Time: 8 to 10 Hours

*Heather Spring
Sheppard Air Force
Base, Texas*
*Entertaining doesn't
get much easier than
when you serve this tasty
five-ingredient entree.*

1/2 cup packed brown sugar
1 teaspoon ground mustard
1 teaspoon prepared
   horseradish
4 tablespoons regular cola,
   divided
1 boneless smoked ham
   (5 to 6 pounds), cut in half

In a bowl, combine the brown sugar, mustard, horseradish and 2 tablespoons cola; mix well. Rub over ham. Place in a 5-qt. slow cooker; pour remaining cola over ham.

Cover and cook on low for 8-10 hours or until a meat thermometer reads 140°. **Yield:** 15-20 servings.

PEACHY PORK STEAKS

Cook Time: 5 Hours

*Sandra McKenzie
Braham, Minnesota*
*My mother has been
preparing this delicious
pork dish for many
years. She always found
it a surefire way to get
even picky children to
eat meat. It seems that
no one can refuse these
succulent steaks!*

4 pork steaks (1/2 inch thick),
   trimmed
2 tablespoons vegetable oil
3/4 teaspoon dried basil
1/4 teaspoon salt
Dash pepper
1 can (15-1/4 ounces) peach
   slices in heavy syrup,
   undrained
2 tablespoons vinegar
1 tablespoon beef bouillon
   granules
2 tablespoons cornstarch
1/4 cup cold water
Hot cooked rice

In a skillet, brown steaks in oil; sprinkle with basil, salt and pepper. Drain peaches; reserve juice. Place peaches in a slow cooker; top with steaks. Combine reserved juice, vinegar and bouillon; pour over steaks. Cover; cook on high 1 hour. Reduce heat to low and cook 4 hours longer or until meat is tender. Remove steaks and peaches to a serving platter; keep warm.

Skim and discard fat from cooking liquid; pour into a saucepan. Combine cornstarch and cold water until smooth; stir into cooking liquid. Bring to a boil; cook and stir 2 minutes. Serve steaks, peaches and sauce over rice. **Yield:** 4 servings.

Slow-Cooked Ham

Spaghetti Pork Chops

SPAGHETTI PORK CHOPS

Cook Time: 6 to 8 Hours

3 cans (8 ounces *each*) tomato
   sauce
1 can (10-3/4 ounces) condensed
   tomato soup, undiluted
1 small onion, finely chopped
1 bay leaf
1 teaspoon celery seed
1/2 teaspoon Italian seasoning
6 bone-in pork chops (1 inch
   thick)
2 tablespoons olive oil
Hot cooked spaghetti

In a 5-qt. slow cooker, combine the tomato sauce, soup, onion, bay leaf, celery seed and Italian seasoning. In a large skillet, brown pork chops in oil. Add to the slow cooker.

Cover and cook on low for 6-8 hours or until meat is tender. Discard bay leaf. Serve chops and sauce over spaghetti. **Yield:** 6 servings.

Ellen Gallavan
Midland, Michigan
In this succulent pork supper, the moist chops simmer to perfection in a tangy sauce, then they are served over pasta.

HAM AND HASH BROWNS

Cook Time: 7 to 8 Hours

1 package (28 ounces) frozen
   O'Brien hash brown potatoes
2 cups cubed fully cooked ham
1 jar (2 ounces) diced pimientos,
   drained
1 can (10-3/4 ounces) condensed
   cheddar cheese soup,
   undiluted
3/4 cup milk
1/4 teaspoon pepper

In a slow cooker, combine the potatoes, ham and pimientos. In a bowl, combine soup, milk and pepper; pour over the potato mixture.

Cover and cook on low for 7-8 hours or until potatoes are tender. **Yield:** 4 servings.

Marlene Muckenhirn
Delano, Minnesota
You just can't beat the slow cooker for convenience…I use mine two or three times a week all year-round. This is a new way to prepare an old-fashioned favorite.

Cranberry Pork Chops

CRANBERRY PORK CHOPS

Cook Time: 7 to 8 Hours

6 bone-in pork loin chops
1 can (16 ounces) jellied
    cranberry sauce
1/2 cup cranberry *or* apple juice
1/4 cup sugar
2 tablespoons spicy brown
    mustard
2 tablespoons cornstarch
1/4 cup cold water
1/2 teaspoon salt
Dash pepper

Place pork chops in a slow cooker. Combine the cranberry sauce, juice, sugar and mustard until smooth; pour over chops. Cover and cook on low for 7-8 hours or until the meat is tender. Remove chops; keep warm.

In a saucepan, combine the cornstarch and cold water until smooth; gradually stir in cooking juices. Bring to a boil; cook and stir for 2 minutes or until thickened. Stir in salt and pepper. Serve over chops. **Yield:** 6 servings.

*Robin Czacnor
Appleton, Wisconsin
My family raves over these chops. Use the mild sweet-and-sour sauce to make a gravy for mashed potatoes. Add a salad and you have a great meal that didn't keep you in the kitchen for hours.*

SHRIMP MARINARA

Cook Time: 3-1/2 to 4-1/2 Hours

1 can (14-1/2 ounces) Italian
    diced tomatoes, undrained
1 can (6 ounces) tomato paste
1/2 to 1 cup water
2 garlic cloves, minced
2 tablespoons minced fresh
    parsley
1 teaspoon salt, optional
1 teaspoon dried oregano
1/2 teaspoon dried basil
1/4 teaspoon pepper
1 pound fresh *or* frozen shrimp,
    cooked, peeled and deveined
1 pound spaghetti, cooked and
    drained
Shredded Parmesan cheese, optional

In a slow cooker, combine the first nine ingredients. Cover and cook on low for 3-4 hours.

Stir in shrimp. Cover and cook 20 minutes longer or just until shrimp are heated through. Serve over spaghetti. Garnish with Parmesan cheese if desired. **Yield:** 6 servings.

*Sue Mackey
Galesburg, Illinois
I simmer this flavorful marinara sauce for most of the day. Then shortly before mealtime, I simply add cooked shrimp, which merely require being heated through. Served over spaghetti, it makes a delicious dressed-up main dish.*

PORK CARNITAS

Cook Time: 9 to 11 Hours

Tracy Byers
Corvallis, Oregon
I use this recipe often when entertaining. I set out all the toppings, and folks have fun assembling their own carnitas. Because I can prepare everything in advance, I get to spend more time with my guests.

1 boneless pork shoulder *or* loin roast (2 to 3 pounds), trimmed and cut into 3-inch cubes
1/2 cup lime juice
1 teaspoon salt
1/2 teaspoon pepper
1/2 teaspoon crushed red pepper flakes
12 flour tortillas (7 inches), warmed
2 cups (8 ounces) shredded cheddar *or* Monterey Jack cheese
2 medium avocados, peeled and diced
2 medium tomatoes, diced
1 medium onion, diced
Shredded lettuce
Minced fresh cilantro, optional
Salsa

In a slow cooker, combine the pork, lime juice, salt, pepper and pepper flakes. Cover and cook on high for 1 hour; stir. Reduce heat to low and cook 8-10 hours longer or until the meat is very tender.

Shred the pork with a fork (it may look somewhat pink). Spoon about 1/3 cup of filling down the center of each tortilla. Top with cheese, avocados, tomatoes, onion, lettuce and cilantro if desired. Fold in bottom and sides of tortilla. Serve with salsa. **Yield:** 12 servings.

SIDE DISHES & CONDIMENTS

CHAPTER 7

Slow Cooker Mashed Potatoes

SLOW COOKER MASHED POTATOES

Cook Time: 2 to 4 Hours

1 package (3 ounces) cream
  cheese, softened
1/2 cup sour cream
1/4 cup butter, softened
1 envelope ranch salad dressing
  mix
1 teaspoon dried parsley flakes
6 cups warm mashed potatoes
  (prepared without milk *or*
  butter)

In a bowl, combine the cream cheese, sour cream, butter, salad dressing mix and parsley; stir in potatoes. Transfer to a slow cooker. Cover and cook on low for 2-4 hours. **Yield:** 8-10 servings.

Editor's Note: This recipe was tested with fresh potatoes (not instant) in a slow cooker with heating elements surrounding the unit, not only in the base.

Trudy Vincent
Valles Mines, Missouri
Sour cream and cream cheese give richness to these smooth make-ahead potatoes. They are wonderful for Thanksgiving or Christmas dinner, since there's no last-minute mashing required.

SPICED ACORN SQUASH

Cook Time: 4 Hours

3/4 cup packed brown sugar
1 teaspoon ground cinnamon
1 teaspoon ground nutmeg
2 small acorn squash, halved and
  seeded
3/4 cup raisins
4 tablespoons butter
1/2 cup water

Combine brown sugar, cinnamon and nutmeg; spoon into the squash halves. Sprinkle with raisins. Top each with 1 tablespoon of butter. Wrap each squash half individually in heavy-duty foil; seal tightly. Pour water into a slow cooker. Place the squash, cut side up, in slow cooker (packets may be stacked).

Cover and cook on high for 4 hours or until the squash is tender. Open foil packets carefully to allow steam to escape. **Yield:** 4 servings.

Carol Greco
Centereach, New York
Working full time, I found I didn't always have time to cook the meals my family loved. So I re-created many of our favorites in the slow cooker. This cinnamony treatment for squash is one of them.

Vegetable Medley

Vegetable Medley

4 cups diced peeled potatoes
1-1/2 cups frozen whole kernel corn
    or 1 can (15-1/4 ounces) whole
    kernel corn, drained
4 medium tomatoes, seeded
    and diced
1 cup sliced carrots
1/2 cup chopped onion
3/4 teaspoon salt
1/2 teaspoon sugar
1/2 teaspoon dill weed
1/8 teaspoon pepper

In a slow cooker, combine all ingredients. Cover; cook on low for 5-6 hours or until vegetables are tender. **Yield:** 8 servings.

Terry Maly
Olathe, Kansas
This is a wonderful side dish to make when garden vegetables are plentiful. The colorful combination is a great complement to any entree.

Cheesy Hash Brown Potatoes

2 cans (10-3/4 ounces *each*)
    condensed cheddar cheese
    soup, undiluted
1-1/3 cups buttermilk
2 tablespoons butter, melted
1/2 teaspoon seasoned salt
1/4 teaspoon garlic powder
1/4 teaspoon pepper
1 package (2 pounds) frozen
    cubed hash brown potatoes
1/4 cup grated Parmesan cheese
1 teaspoon paprika

In a slow cooker, combine the first six ingredients; stir in hash browns. Sprinkle with Parmesan cheese and paprika. Cover and cook on low for 4 to 4-1/2 hours or until potatoes are tender. **Yield:** 6-8 servings.

Becky Weseman
Becker, Minnesota
I adapted this recipe for my slow cooker so I could bring these cheesy potatoes to a potluck picnic. Canned soup and frozen hash browns make this dish easy to assemble.

Slow-Simmered Kidney Beans

Slow-Simmered Kidney Beans

Cook Time: 6 to 8 Hours

6 bacon strips, diced

1/2 pound fully cooked kielbasa *or* Polish sausage, chopped

4 cans (16 ounces *each*) kidney beans, rinsed and drained

1 can (28 ounces) diced tomatoes, drained

2 medium sweet red peppers, chopped

1 large onion, chopped

1 cup ketchup

1/2 cup packed brown sugar

1/4 cup honey

1/4 cup molasses

1 tablespoon Worcestershire sauce

1 teaspoon salt

1 teaspoon ground mustard

2 medium unpeeled red apples, cored and cut into 1/2-inch pieces

In a skillet, cook bacon until crisp. Remove with a slotted spoon to paper towels. Add sausage to drippings; cook and stir 5 minutes. Drain; set aside.

In an ungreased 5-qt. slow cooker, combine the beans, tomatoes, red peppers, onion, ketchup, brown sugar, honey, molasses, Worcestershire sauce, salt and mustard. Stir in the bacon and sausage.

Cover and cook on low for 4-6 hours. Stir in the apples. Cover and cook 2 hours longer or until bubbly. **Yield:** 16 servings.

Sheila Vail
Long Beach, California
My husband always puts us down for this side dish when we're invited to a potluck. Canned beans cut down on prep time yet get plenty of zip from bacon, apple, red pepper and onion. I like simmering this mixture in the slow cooker because it blends the flavors and I don't have to stand over the stove.

Michigan Beans and Sausage

Cook Time: 6 to 8 Hours

Janice Lass
Dorr, Michigan
This recipe from a church cookbook caught my eye years ago. Bean casseroles are a big hit at potlucks and picnics.

1 pound fully cooked kielbasa *or* Polish sausage, halved lengthwise and thinly sliced
1 medium onion, chopped
1 cup ketchup
3/4 cup packed brown sugar
1/2 cup sugar
2 tablespoons vinegar
2 tablespoons molasses
2 tablespoons prepared mustard
3 cans (15-1/2 ounces *each*) great northern beans, rinsed and drained

In a saucepan, cook sausage and onion in boiling water for 2 minutes; drain. In a bowl, combine the ketchup, sugars, vinegar, molasses and mustard. Stir in the beans and sausage mixture. Transfer to a slow cooker.

Cover and cook on low for 6-8 hours or until heated through. **Yield:** 14-16 servings.

Spanish Hominy

Cook Time: 6 to 8 Hours

Donna Brockett
Kingfisher, Oklahoma
I received this recipe from a good friend who is known to be a fabulous cook. The colorful side dish gets its zesty flavor from spicy canned tomatoes with green chilies. It's a great way to perk up any main dish.

4 cans (15-1/2 ounces *each*) hominy, drained
1 can (14-1/2 ounces) diced tomatoes, undrained
1 can (10 ounces) diced tomatoes and green chilies, undrained
1 can (8 ounces) tomato sauce
3/4 pound sliced bacon, diced
1 large onion, chopped
1 medium green pepper, chopped

In a slow cooker, combine the hominy, tomatoes and tomato sauce. In a skillet, cook the bacon until crisp; remove with a slotted spoon to paper towels. Drain, reserving 1 tablespoon drippings.

Saute the onion and green pepper in the drippings until tender. Stir onion mixture and bacon into the hominy mixture. Cover; cook on low for 6-8 hours or until heated through. **Yield:** 12 servings.

Michigan Beans and Sausage

LEMON RED POTATOES

Cook Time: 2-1/2 to 3 Hours

Tara Branham
Cedar Park, Texas
Butter, lemon juice,
parsley and chives
enhance simple red
potatoes. Since they
cook in the slow cooker,
there's plenty of room
on the stove for
other dishes.

1-1/2 pounds medium red potatoes
1/4 cup water
1/4 cup butter, melted
1 tablespoon lemon juice
3 tablespoons snipped fresh parsley
1 tablespoon snipped fresh chives
Salt and pepper to taste

Cut a strip of peel from around the middle of each potato. Place potatoes and water in a slow cooker. Cover and cook on high for 2-1/2 to 3 hours or until tender (do not overcook); drain. Combine butter, lemon juice, parsley and chives; mix well. Pour over the potatoes and toss to coat. Season with salt and pepper. **Yield:** 6 servings.

CHEESY CREAMED CORN

Cook Time: 4 Hours

Mary Ann Truit
Wichita, Kansas
My family really likes
this creamy, cheesy side
dish—and it's so easy to
make. Even those who
usually don't eat much
corn will ask for a
second helping.

3 packages (16 ounces *each*) frozen corn
2 packages (one 8 ounces, one 3 ounces) cream cheese, cubed
1/4 cup butter, cubed
3 tablespoons water
3 tablespoons milk
2 tablespoons sugar
6 slices process cheese, cut into small pieces

Combine all ingredients in a slow cooker; mix well. Cover and cook on low for 4 hours or until heated through and the cheese is melted. Stir well before serving. **Yield:** 12 servings.

Lemon Red Potatoes
Cheesy Creamed Corn

Hot Fruit Salad

HOT FRUIT SALAD

Cook Time: 3 to 4 Hours

1 jar (25 ounces) chunky
    applesauce
1 can (21 ounces) cherry pie
    filling
1 can (20 ounces) pineapple
    chunks, undrained
1 can (15-1/4 ounces) sliced
    peaches, undrained
1 can (15-1/4 ounces) apricot
    halves, undrained
1 can (15 ounces) mandarin
    oranges, undrained
1/2 cup packed brown sugar
1 teaspoon ground cinnamon

Place the first six ingredients in a slow cooker and stir gently. Combine brown sugar and cinnamon; sprinkle over fruit mixture. Cover and cook on low for 3-4 hours. **Yield:** 16 servings.

Barb Vande Voort
New Sharon, Iowa
This spicy fruit mixture is a breeze to make— just open the cans and empty them into the slow cooker. With its pretty color from cherry pie filling, this salad is nice for any special occasion.

ALL-DAY APPLE BUTTER

Cook Time: 11 to 13 Hours

5-1/2 pounds apples, peeled and
    finely chopped
4 cups sugar
2 to 3 teaspoons ground
    cinnamon
1/4 teaspoon ground cloves
1/4 teaspoon salt

Place apples in a slow cooker. Combine sugar, cinnamon, cloves and salt; pour over apples and mix well. Cover and cook on high for 1 hour. Reduce heat to low; cover and cook for 9-11 hours or until thickened and dark brown, stirring occasionally (stir more frequently as it thickens to prevent sticking).

Uncover and cook on low 1 hour longer. If desired, stir with a wire whisk until smooth. Spoon into freezer containers, leaving 1/2-in. headspace. Cover and refrigerate or freeze. **Yield:** 4 pints.

Betty Ruenholl
Syracuse, Nebraska
With this spread, the fresh flavor of apples at harvesttime can be enjoyed all year. Depending on the sweetness of the apples used, you can adjust the sugar to taste.

Moist Poultry Dressing

MOIST POULTRY DRESSING

Cook Time: 4 to 5 Hours

2 jars (4-1/2 ounces *each*) sliced
  mushrooms, drained
4 celery ribs, chopped
2 medium onions, chopped
1/4 cup minced fresh parsley
3/4 cup butter
1-1/2 pounds day-old bread,
  crusts removed and cubed
  (about 13 cups)
1-1/2 teaspoons salt
1-1/2 teaspoons rubbed sage
1 teaspoon poultry seasoning
1 teaspoon dried thyme
1/2 teaspoon pepper

2 eggs
1 can (14-1/2 ounces) chicken
  broth

In a large skillet, saute the mushrooms, celery, onions and parsley in butter until the vegetables are tender.

In a large bowl, toss the bread cubes with salt, sage, poultry seasoning, thyme and pepper. Add the mushroom mixture. Combine eggs and broth; add to the bread mixture and toss. Transfer to a slow cooker.

Cover and cook on low for 4-5 hours or until a meat thermometer reads 160°. **Yield:** 12-16 servings.

Ruth Ann Stelfox
Raymond, Alberta
Tasty mushrooms and onions complement the big herb flavor in this dressing. Every forkful stays wonderfully moist when cooked this way.

SLOW-COOKED SAGE DRESSING

Cook Time: 4 to 5 Hours

14 to 15 cups day-old bread
  cubes
3 cups chopped celery
1-1/2 cups chopped onion
1-1/2 teaspoons rubbed sage
1 teaspoon salt
1/2 teaspoon pepper
1-1/4 cups butter, melted

Combine bread, celery, onion, sage, salt and pepper; mix well. Add butter and toss. Spoon into a 5-qt. slow cooker. Cover and cook on low for 4-5 hours, stirring once. **Yield:** about 12 servings.

Ellen Benninger
Stoneboro, Pennsylvania
This recipe is such a help at holidaytime. There's room in the oven for other dishes when this simple yet delicious dressing is fixed in the slow cooker.

Chunky Applesauce

CHUNKY APPLESAUCE

Cook Time: 6 to 8 Hours

8 to 10 large tart apples, peeled
and cut into chunks
1/2 to 1 cup sugar
1/2 cup water
1 teaspoon ground cinnamon

Combine apples, sugar, water and cinnamon in a slow cooker; stir gently. Cover and cook on low for 6-8 hours or until apples are tender. **Yield:** 5 cups.

Lisa Roessner
Ft. Recovery, Ohio
I'm so glad my mother gave me the recipe for this warm and cinnamony apple dish. Simmering it in a slow cooker fills the house with a wonderful aroma.

HOT GERMAN POTATO SALAD

Cook Time: 4 to 5 Hours

8 medium potatoes, peeled
and cut into 1/4-inch slices
2 celery ribs, chopped
1 large onion, chopped
1 cup water
2/3 cup cider vinegar
1/3 cup sugar
2 tablespoons quick-cooking
tapioca
1 teaspoon salt
3/4 teaspoon celery seed
1/4 teaspoon pepper
6 bacon strips, cooked and
crumbled
1/4 cup minced fresh parsley

In a slow cooker, combine the potatoes, celery and onion. In a bowl, combine the water, vinegar, sugar, tapioca, salt, celery seed and pepper. Pour over the potatoes; stir gently to coat.

Cover and cook on high for 4-5 hours or until potatoes are tender. Just before serving, sprinkle with bacon and parsley. **Yield:** 8-10 servings.

Marlene Muckenhirn
Delano, Minnesota
I make this zesty salad with potatoes, celery and onion. It's a terrific side dish when served warm with crumbled bacon and fresh parsley sprinkled on top.

PARTYTIME BEANS

Cook Time: 5 to 7 Hours

Jean Cantner
Boston, Virginia
A friend brought this colorful bean dish to my house for a church circle potluck dinner. As soon as I tasted these slightly sweet baked beans, I had to have the recipe. I've served this and shared the recipe many times since.

1-1/2 cups ketchup
1 medium onion, chopped
1 medium green pepper, chopped
1 medium sweet red pepper, chopped
1/2 cup water
1/2 cup packed brown sugar
2 bay leaves
2 to 3 teaspoons cider vinegar
1 teaspoon ground mustard
1/8 teaspoon pepper
1 can (16 ounces) kidney beans, rinsed and drained
1 can (15-1/2 ounces) great northern beans, rinsed and drained
1 can (15 ounces) lima beans, rinsed and drained
1 can (15 ounces) black beans, rinsed and drained
1 can (15-1/2 ounces) black-eyed peas, rinsed and drained

In a slow cooker, combine the first 10 ingredients; mix well. Add the beans and peas; mix well. Cover and cook on low for 5-7 hours or until onion and peppers are tender. Remove bay leaves. **Yield:** 14-16 servings.

LAZY-DAY CRANBERRY RELISH

Cook Time: 6 Hours

June Formanek
Belle Plaine, Iowa
When I get busy with holiday bustle, this no-fuss, ruby-red condiment can be simmering in my kitchen.

2 cups sugar
1 cup orange juice
1 teaspoon grated orange peel
4 cups fresh *or* frozen cranberries

In a slow cooker, combine sugar, orange juice and peel; stir until sugar is dissolved. Add the cranberries. Cover and cook on low for 6 hours. Mash the mixture. Chill several hours or overnight. **Yield:** 10-12 servings (3 cups).

Partytime Beans

CREAMY HASH BROWNS

Cook Time: 4 to 5 Hours

Donna Downes
Las Vegas, Nevada
My mother often took this comforting side dish to social dinners because it was such a hit. Now I get the same compliments when I make it. The popular flavors of bacon and onion jazz up a creamy hash brown mixture.

1 package (2 pounds) frozen cubed hash brown potatoes
2 cups (8 ounces) cubed process cheese (Velveeta)
2 cups (16 ounces) sour cream
1 can (10-3/4 ounces) condensed cream of celery soup, undiluted
1 can (10-3/4 ounces) condensed cream of chicken soup, undiluted
1 pound sliced bacon, cooked and crumbled

1 large onion, chopped
1/4 cup butter, melted
1/4 teaspoon pepper

Place potatoes in an ungreased 5-qt. slow cooker. In a bowl, combine the remaining ingredients. Pour over potatoes and mix well.

Cover and cook on low for 4-5 hours or until potatoes are tender and heated through. **Yield:** 14 servings.

CHEESY SPINACH

Cook Time: 5 to 6 Hours

Frances Moore
Decatur, Illinois
My daughter often serves this cheese and spinach blend at church suppers. She always comes home with an empty slow cooker. Everyone likes this flavorful combination once they try it.

2 packages (10 ounces *each*) frozen chopped spinach, thawed and well drained
2 cups (16 ounces) small-curd cottage cheese
1-1/2 cups cubed process cheese (Velveeta)
3 eggs, lightly beaten
1/4 cup butter, cubed
1/4 cup all-purpose flour
1 teaspoon salt

In a large bowl, combine all ingredients. Pour into a greased slow cooker. Cover and cook on high for 1 hour. Reduce heat to low; cook 4-5 hours longer or until a knife inserted near the center comes out clean. **Yield:** 6-8 servings.

Creamy Hash Browns

SLOW-COOKED BROCCOLI

Cook Time: 2-1/2 to 3 Hours

Connie Slocum
St. Simons Island,
Georgia
This casserole is quick to assemble and full of good flavor. Even those who don't usually like broccoli enjoy it served this way. I can also serve this dish in the summer alongside grilled meat, since it doesn't heat up the house as it cooks.

2 packages (10 ounces *each*) frozen chopped broccoli, partially thawed
1 can (10-3/4 ounces) condensed cream of celery soup, undiluted
1-1/2 cups (6 ounces) shredded sharp cheddar cheese, *divided*
1/4 cup chopped onion
1/2 teaspoon Worcestershire sauce
1/4 teaspoon pepper
1 cup crushed butter-flavored crackers (about 25 crackers)
2 tablespoons butter

In a large bowl, combine the broccoli, soup, 1 cup cheese, onion, Worcestershire sauce and pepper. Pour into a greased slow cooker. Sprinkle crackers on top; dot with butter.

Cover and cook on high for 2-1/2 to 3 hours. Sprinkle with remaining cheese. Cook 10 minutes longer or until the cheese is melted. **Yield:** 8-10 servings.

SIMPLE SAUCY POTATOES

Cook Time: 4 to 5 Hours

Gloria Schroeder
Ottawa Lake, Michigan
These rich and creamy potatoes are easy to prepare for potlucks and holiday meals. This saucy side dish always gets rave reviews wherever I take it.

4 cans (15 ounces *each*) sliced white potatoes, drained
2 cans (10-3/4 ounces *each*) condensed cream of celery soup, undiluted
2 cups (16 ounces) sour cream
10 bacon strips, cooked and crumbled
6 green onions, thinly sliced

Place potatoes in a slow cooker. Combine the remaining ingredients; pour over potatoes and mix well. Cover and cook on high for 4-5 hours. **Yield:** 12 servings.

Slow-Cooked Broccoli

Sweet 'n' Sour Beans

Cook Time: 3 to 4 Hours

Barbara Short
Mena, Arkansas
This recipe is popular on both sides of the border. It came from a friend in Alaska, then traveled with me to Mexico, where I lived for 5 years, and is now a potluck favorite in my Arkansas community. It's easy to keep the beans warm and serve from a slow cooker.

8 bacon strips, diced
2 medium onions, halved and thinly sliced
1 cup packed brown sugar
1/2 cup cider vinegar
1 teaspoon salt
1 teaspoon ground mustard
1/2 teaspoon garlic powder
1 can (28 ounces) baked beans, undrained
1 can (16 ounces) kidney beans, rinsed and drained
1 can (15-1/2 ounces) pinto beans, rinsed and drained
1 can (15 ounces) lima beans, rinsed and drained
1 can (15-1/2 ounces) black-eyed peas, rinsed and drained

In a large skillet, cook bacon until crisp. Remove to paper towels. Drain, reserving 2 tablespoons drippings. In the drippings, saute onions until tender. Add brown sugar, vinegar, salt, mustard and garlic powder. Bring to a boil.

In a slow cooker, combine beans and peas. Add onion mixture and bacon; mix well. Cover and cook on high for 3-4 hours or until heated through. **Yield:** 15-20 servings.

Sweet 'n' Sour Beans

Creamy Red Potatoes

CREAMY RED POTATOES

Cook Time: 5 to 6 Hours

7 cups cubed uncooked red
  potatoes
1 cup (8 ounces) small-curd
  cottage cheese
1/2 cup sour cream
1/2 cup cubed process cheese
  (Velveeta)
1 tablespoon dried minced
  onion
2 garlic cloves, minced
1/2 teaspoon salt
Paprika and minced chives, optional

Place potatoes in a slow cooker. In a blender or food processor, puree cottage cheese and sour cream until smooth. Transfer to a bowl; stir in the process cheese, onion, garlic and salt. Pour over potatoes and mix well.

Cover and cook on low for 5-6 hours or until potatoes are tender. Stir well before serving. Garnish with paprika and chives if desired. **Yield:** 8 servings.

Elaine Ryan
Holley, New York
This side dish features cubed red potatoes that are cooked in a creamy coating until tender. Be sure to stir the mixture before serving to help the sauce thicken.

SLOW-COOKED VEGETABLES

Cook Time: 7 to 8 Hours

4 celery ribs, cut into 1-inch
  pieces
4 small carrots, cut into 1-inch
  pieces
2 medium tomatoes, cut into
  chunks
2 medium onions, thinly sliced
2 cups cut fresh green beans
  (1-inch pieces)
1 medium green pepper, cut
  into 1-inch pieces
1/4 cup butter, melted

3 tablespoons quick-cooking
  tapioca
1 tablespoon sugar
2 teaspoons salt
1/8 teaspoon pepper

Place the vegetables in a slow cooker. Combine butter, tapioca, sugar, salt and pepper; pour over vegetables and stir well. Cover and cook on low for 7-8 hours or until vegetables are tender. Serve with a slotted spoon. **Yield:** 8 servings.

Kathy Westendorf
Westgate, Iowa
I simmer a variety of garden-fresh vegetables into this satisfying side dish. My sister-in-law shared this recipe with me. It's a favorite at holiday gatherings and potlucks.

Slow-Cooked Mac 'n' Cheese

SLOW-COOKED MAC 'N' CHEESE

Cook Time: 4-1/2 Hours

1 package (16 ounces) elbow
  macaroni
1/2 cup butter, melted
2 eggs, beaten
1 can (12 ounces) evaporated
  milk
1 can (10-3/4 ounces) condensed
  cheddar cheese soup,
  undiluted
1 cup milk
4 cups (16 ounces) shredded
  cheddar cheese, *divided*
1/8 teaspoon paprika

Cook macaroni according to package directions; drain. Place in a 5-qt. slow cooker; add butter. In a bowl, combine the eggs, evaporated milk, soup, milk and 3 cups cheese. Pour over macaroni mixture; stir to combine.

Cover and cook on low for 4 hours. Sprinkle with the remaining cheese. Cook 15 minutes longer or until cheese is melted. Sprinkle with paprika. **Yield:** 10 servings.

Bernice Glascoe
Roxboro,
North Carolina
This cheesy classic casserole is a great way to spark satisfied smiles around the table. It's homespun comfort food that goes well with any meat and is even rich and filling enough to be the entree.

PINEAPPLE SWEET POTATOES

Cook Time: 4 to 5 Hours

6 to 6-1/2 cups mashed sweet
  potatoes (without added milk
  and butter)
4 eggs
1 cup milk
1/2 cup butter, softened
1 teaspoon vanilla extract
1/2 teaspoon lemon extract
1 teaspoon salt
1 teaspoon ground cinnamon
1/2 teaspoon ground nutmeg

1 can (8 ounces) pineapple slices,
  drained
1/4 cup chopped pecans

In a mixing bowl, combine the first nine ingredients; mix well. Transfer to a slow cooker. Top with pineapple slices and pecans. Cover and cook on low for 4-5 hours or until a thermometer reads 160°. **Yield:** 12-14 servings.

Bette Fulcher
Lexington, Texas
Pineapple and pecans make a pretty topping for this no-fuss fall side dish. It's light, tasty and not too sweet. Making it in the slow cooker leaves extra space in the oven when preparing a holiday dinner.

Slow-Cooked Beans

Slow-Cooked Beans

Cook Time: 2 Hours

4 cans (15-1/2 ounces *each*) great northern beans, rinsed and drained
4 cans (15 ounces *each*) black beans, rinsed and drained
2 cans (15 ounces *each*) butter beans, rinsed and drained
2-1/4 cups barbecue sauce
2-1/4 cups salsa
3/4 cup packed brown sugar
1/2 to 1 teaspoon hot pepper sauce

In a 5-qt. slow cooker, gently combine all ingredients. Cover and cook on low for 2 hours or until heated through. **Yield:** 16 servings.

Joy Beck
Cincinnati, Ohio
This flavorful bean dish adds nice variety to any buffet. It's different from more traditional baked beans. It's a snap to prepare, too.

Potato Hot Dish

Cook Time: 8 to 10 Hours

6 medium potatoes, peeled and cut into 1/4-inch strips
2 cups (8 ounces) shredded cheddar cheese
1 can (10-3/4 ounces) condensed cream of chicken soup, undiluted
1 small onion, chopped *or* 1 tablespoon dried minced onion
7 tablespoons butter, melted, *divided*
1 teaspoon salt
1 teaspoon pepper
1 cup (8 ounces) sour cream
2 cups seasoned stuffing cubes

Toss the potatoes and cheese; place in a 5-qt. slow cooker. Combine soup, onion, 4 tablespoons butter, salt and pepper; pour over potato mixture.

Cover and cook on low for 8-10 hours or until potatoes are tender. Stir in sour cream. Toss stuffing cubes and remaining butter; sprinkle over potatoes. **Yield:** 10-12 servings.

Melissa Marzolf
Marysville, Michigan
For a comforting side dish that feeds a crowd, try these saucy slow-cooked potatoes. A topping of buttered croutons covers the creamy combination.

FOUR-BEAN MEDLEY

Cook Time: 6 to 7 Hours

Susanne Wasson
Montgomery, New York
This bean side dish will draw compliments. It's a hearty and great-tasting addition to any meal. Because it's easy to fix ahead and simmer in the slow cooker, it's convenient to take to potluck dinners and church meals.

8 bacon strips, diced
2 medium onions, quartered and sliced
3/4 cup packed brown sugar
1/2 cup vinegar
1 teaspoon salt
1 teaspoon ground mustard
1/2 teaspoon garlic powder
1 can (16 ounces) baked beans, undrained
1 can (16 ounces) kidney beans, rinsed and drained
1 can (15-1/2 ounces) butter beans, rinsed and drained
1 can (14-1/2 ounces) cut green beans, drained

In a skillet, cook bacon until crisp. Drain, reserving 2 tablespoons drippings; set bacon aside. Saute onions in drippings until tender. Stir in brown sugar, vinegar, salt, mustard and garlic powder. Simmer, uncovered, for 15 minutes or until the onions are golden brown.

Combine the beans in a slow cooker. Add onion mixture and bacon; mix well. Cover and cook on low for 6-7 hours or until the beans are tender. Serve with a slotted spoon. **Yield:** 8-10 servings.

MUSHROOM WILD RICE

Cook Time: 7 to 8 Hours

Bob Malchow
Monon, Indiana
This is one of my favorite recipes from my mother. With only seven ingredients, it's quick to assemble in the morning before I leave for work.

2-1/4 cups water
1 can (10-1/2 ounces) condensed beef consomme, undiluted
1 can (10-1/2 ounces) condensed French onion soup, undiluted
3 cans (4 ounces *each*) mushroom stems and pieces, drained
1/2 cup butter, melted
1 cup uncooked brown rice
1 cup uncooked wild rice

In a slow cooker, combine all ingredients; stir well. Cover and cook on low for 7-8 hours or until rice is tender. **Yield:** 12-16 servings.

SWEET ENDINGS

CHAPTER 8

Nutty Apple Streusel Dessert

Cook Time: 6 to 7 Hours

Jacki Every
Rotterdam, New York
Many people don't think of using a slow cooker to make dessert, but I like finishing up our dinner and having this hot, scrumptious apple treat waiting to be served up. I can start it in the morning and not think about it all day.

6 cups sliced peeled tart apples
1-1/4 teaspoons ground cinnamon
1/4 teaspoon ground allspice
1/4 teaspoon ground nutmeg
3/4 cup milk
2 tablespoons butter, softened
3/4 cup sugar
2 eggs
1 teaspoon vanilla extract
1/2 cup biscuit/baking mix
TOPPING:
1 cup biscuit/baking mix
1/3 cup packed brown sugar
3 tablespoons cold butter
1/2 cup sliced almonds
Ice cream *or* whipped cream, optional

In a large bowl, toss apples with cinnamon, allspice and nutmeg. Place in a greased slow cooker. In a mixing bowl, combine milk, butter, sugar, eggs, vanilla and baking mix; mix well. Spoon over apples.

For topping, combine the biscuit mix and brown sugar in a bowl; cut in butter until crumbly. Add almonds; sprinkle over the apples.

Cover and cook on low for 6-7 hours or until the apples are tender. Serve with ice cream or whipped cream if desired. **Yield:** 6-8 servings.

Nutty Apple Streusel Dessert

Black and Blue Cobbler

Martha Creveling
Orlando, Florida
One day, I decided to try my favorite fruity dessert recipe in the slow cooker. It took a bit of experimenting, but the results are "berry" well worth it.

1 cup all-purpose flour
1-1/2 cups sugar, *divided*
1 teaspoon baking powder
1/4 teaspoon salt
1/4 teaspoon ground cinnamon
1/4 teaspoon ground nutmeg
2 eggs, beaten
2 tablespoons milk
2 tablespoons vegetable oil
2 cups fresh *or* frozen blackberries
2 cups fresh *or* frozen blueberries
3/4 cup water
1 teaspoon grated orange peel
Whipped cream *or* ice cream, optional

In a bowl, combine flour, 3/4 cup sugar, baking powder, salt, cinnamon and nutmeg. Combine eggs, milk and oil; stir into dry ingredients just until moistened. Spread the batter evenly onto the bottom of a greased 5-qt. slow cooker. In a saucepan, combine berries, water, orange peel and remaining sugar; bring to a boil. Remove from the heat; immediately pour over batter.

Cover and cook on high for 2 to 2-1/2 hours or until a toothpick inserted into the batter comes out clean. Turn cooker off. Uncover and let stand for 30 minutes before serving. Serve with whipped cream or ice cream if desired. **Yield:** 6 servings.

Minister's Delight

Mary Ann Potte
Blue Springs, Missouri
A friend gave me this recipe. She said a local minister's wife fixed it every Sunday, so she named it accordingly.

1 can (21 ounces) cherry *or* apple pie filling
1 package (18-1/4 ounces) yellow cake mix
1/2 cup butter, melted
1/3 cup chopped walnuts, optional

Place pie filling in a slow cooker. Combine dry cake mix and butter (mixture will be crumbly); sprinkle over filling. Sprinkle with walnuts if desired. Cover and cook on low for 2-3 hours. Serve in bowls. **Yield:** 10-12 servings.

Black and Blue Cobbler

Fruit Dessert Topping

FRUIT DESSERT TOPPING

Cook Time: 3-1/2 to 4-1/2 Hours

3 medium tart apples, peeled and sliced
3 medium pears, peeled and sliced
1 tablespoon lemon juice
1/2 cup packed brown sugar
1/2 cup maple syrup
1/4 cup butter, melted
1/2 cup chopped pecans
1/4 cup raisins
2 cinnamon sticks (3 inches)
1 tablespoon cornstarch
2 tablespoons cold water
Pound cake *or* ice cream

In a slow cooker, toss the apples and pears with the lemon juice. Combine the brown sugar, maple syrup and butter; pour over fruit. Stir in the pecans, raisins and cinnamon sticks. Cover and cook on low for 3-4 hours.

Combine the cornstarch and water until smooth; gradually stir into slow cooker. Cover and cook on high for 30-40 minutes or until thickened. Discard cinnamon sticks. Serve over pound cake or ice cream. **Yield:** about 6 cups.

Doris Heath
Franklin,
North Carolina
You'll quickly warm up to the down-home flavor of this fruit topping. Spoon it over vanilla ice cream or slices of pound cake.

SLOW COOKER BREAD PUDDING

Cook Time: 3 Hours

8 cups cubed day-old unfrosted cinnamon rolls
2 cups milk
4 eggs
1/4 cup sugar
1/4 cup butter, melted
1/2 teaspoon vanilla extract
1/4 teaspoon ground nutmeg
1 cup raisins

Place cubed cinnamon rolls in a slow cooker. In a mixing bowl, combine the next six ingredients; beat until smooth. Stir in raisins. Pour over cinnamon rolls; stir gently. Cover and cook on low for 3 hours. **Yield:** 6 servings.

Editor's Note: 8 slices of cinnamon or white bread, cut into 1-inch cubes, may be substituted for the cinnamon rolls.

Edna Hoffman
Hebron, Indiana
Use a slow cooker to turn day-old cinnamon rolls into a comforting, old-fashioned dessert. It tastes wonderful topped with lemon or vanilla sauce or whipped cream.

Pumpkin Pie Pudding

PUMPKIN PIE PUDDING

Cook Time: 6 to 7 Hours

1 can (15 ounces) solid-pack
  pumpkin
1 can (12 ounces) evaporated
  milk
3/4 cup sugar
1/2 cup biscuit/baking mix
2 eggs, beaten
2 tablespoons butter, melted
2-1/2 teaspoons pumpkin pie spice
2 teaspoons vanilla extract
Whipped topping, optional

In a large bowl, combine the first eight ingredients. Transfer to a slow cooker coated with nonstick cooking spray.

Cover and cook on low for 6-7 hours or until a thermometer reads 160°. Serve in bowls with whipped topping if desired. **Yield:** 6-8 servings.

Andrea Schaak
Bloomington,
Minnesota
My husband loves anything pumpkin, and this creamy, comforting dessert is one of his favorites. We make this super-easy pudding year-round, but it's especially nice in fall.

CHOCOLATE PUDDING CAKE

Cook Time: 6 to 7 Hours

1 package (18-1/4 ounces)
  chocolate cake mix
1 package (3.9 ounces) instant
  chocolate pudding mix
2 cups (16 ounces) sour cream
4 eggs
1 cup water
3/4 cup vegetable oil
1 cup (6 ounces) semisweet
  chocolate chips
Whipped cream *or* ice cream,
  optional

In a mixing bowl, combine the first six ingredients. Beat on medium speed for 2 minutes. Stir in chocolate chips. Pour into a 5-qt. slow cooker coated with nonstick cooking spray.

Cover and cook on low for 6-7 hours or until a toothpick inserted near the center comes out with moist crumbs. Serve in bowls with whipped cream or ice cream if desired. **Yield:** 10-12 servings.

Paige Arnette
Lawrenceville, Georgia
This recipe makes a rich, fudgy dessert that's a cross between pudding and cake. I like to serve this scrumptious treat warm with a scoop of vanilla ice cream. Whenever I take it to parties, everybody wants the recipe.

Heroes like the Super Friends have many enemies. To protect the world, Superman has to face powerful super-villains.

Lex Luthor is an evil super-genius who wants to destroy the Man of Steel. But Lex isn't smart enough to realize that Superman can get out of any sticky situation this villain dreams up!

General Zod is also from the planet Krypton. He has the same incredible powers as Superman.

But this vain villain is no match for Superman, who uses brains as well as brawn to stop Zod every time!

Brainiac travels from galaxy to galaxy, shrinking entire cities to put in his private library!

But even Brainiac's sophisticated science isn't enough to make Superman part of his collection.

Mr. Mxyzptlk comes from the magical Fifth Dimension. This strange little man can make anything happen! The only way to get rid of this impossible pest is to make him say his name backward.

Can you help Mr. Mxyzptlk read the sign Superman is holding? "Good work, little hero!" Superman says.

Superman and the Super Friends are always ready to defend Earth. With their combined abilities, there is no threat too big for them to handle. And there are some very **BIG** threats!

And when the world is safe again, Superman flies off, always ready for his next adventure.

"Up, up, and away!"